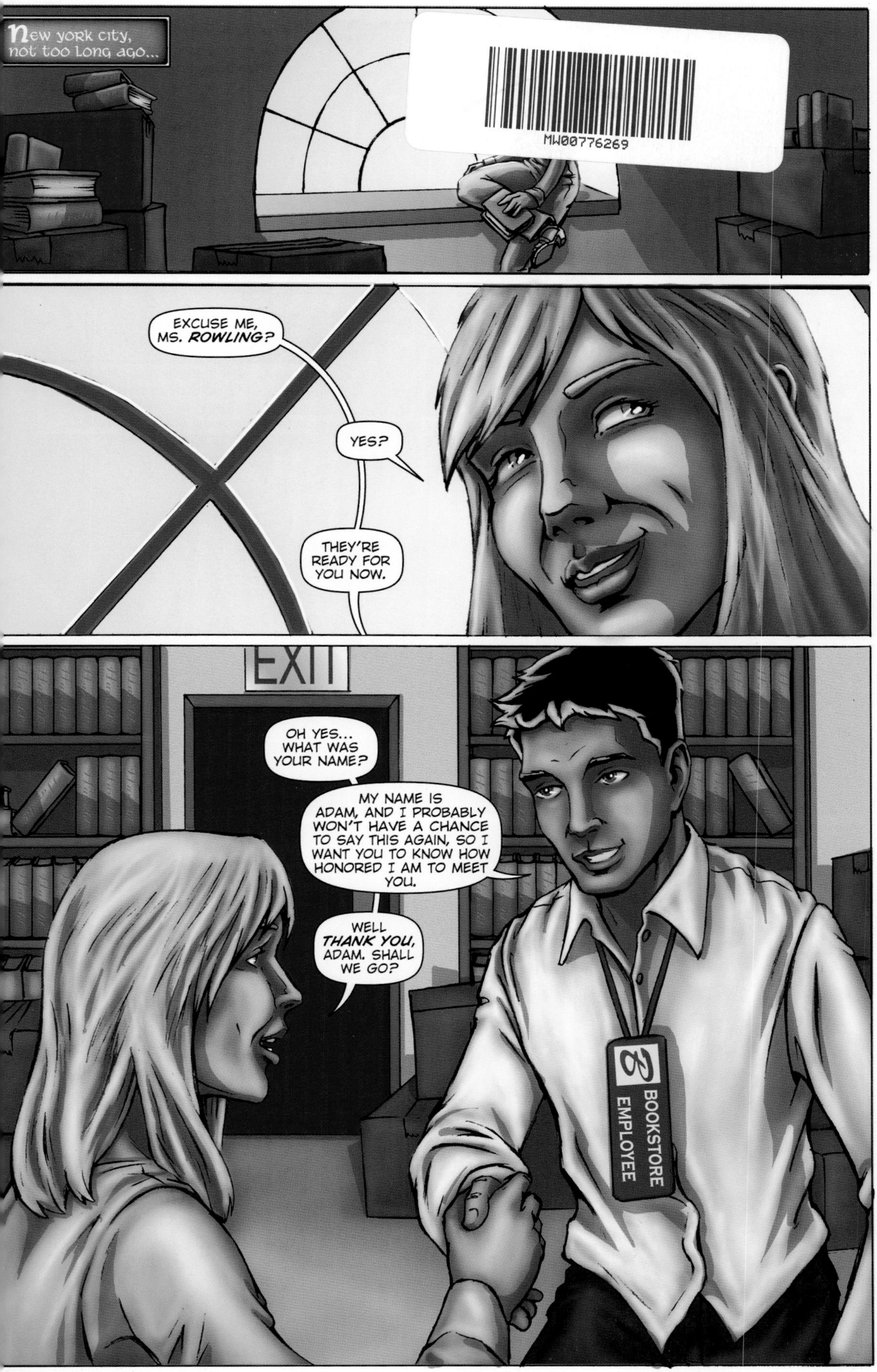
New york city, not too long ago...
EXCUSE ME, MS. ROWLING?
YES?
THEY'RE READY FOR YOU NOW.
EXIT
OH YES... WHAT WAS YOUR NAME?
MY NAME IS ADAM, AND I PROBABLY WON'T HAVE A CHANCE TO SAY THIS AGAIN, SO I WANT YOU TO KNOW HOW HONORED I AM TO MEET YOU.
WELL THANK YOU, ADAM. SHALL WE GO?
BOOKSTORE EMPLOYEE

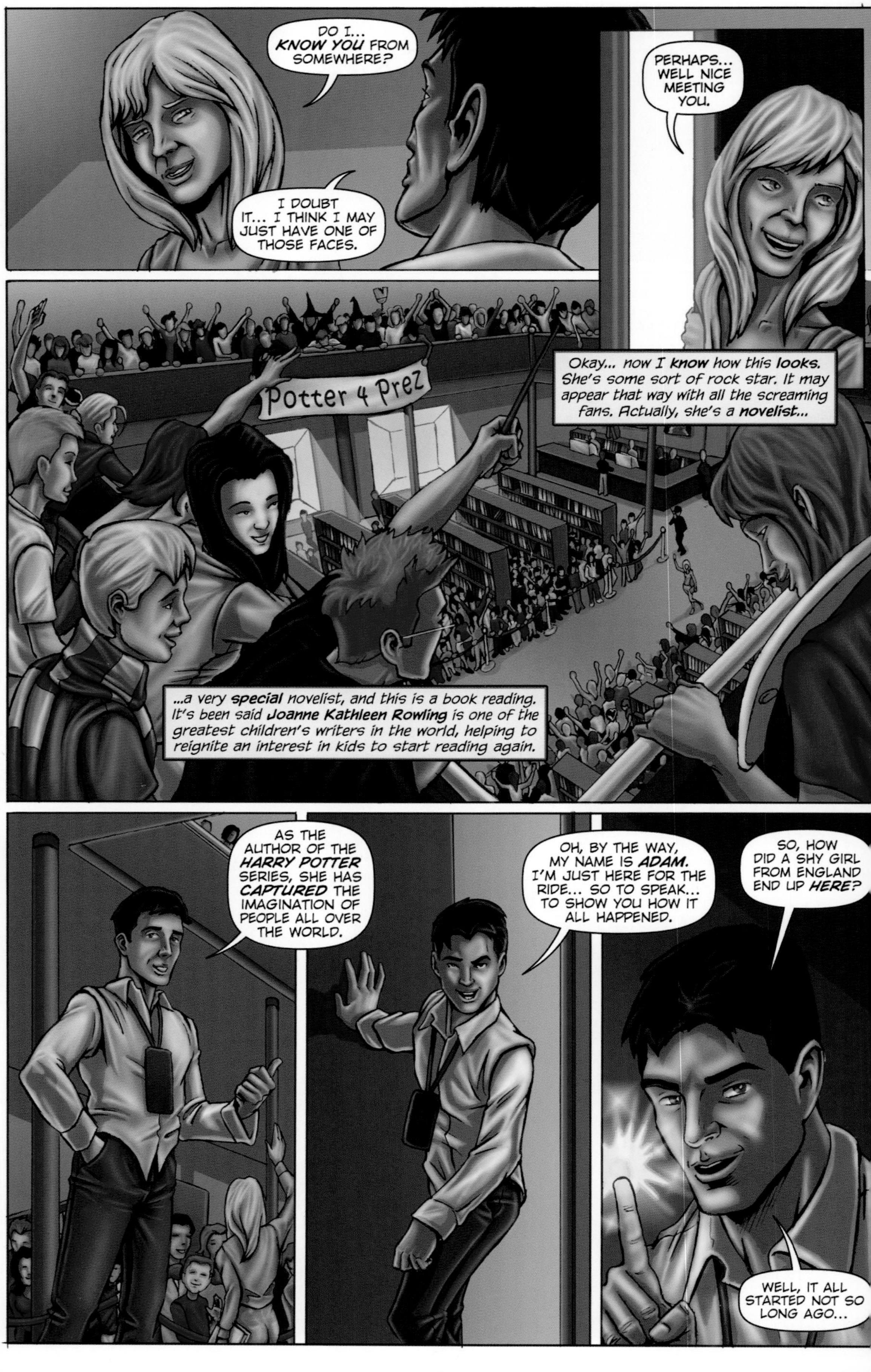

DO I... KNOW YOU FROM SOMEWHERE?
I DOUBT IT... I THINK I MAY JUST HAVE ONE OF THOSE FACES.
PERHAPS... WELL NICE MEETING YOU.
Potter 4 Prez
Okay... now I know how this looks. She's some sort of rock star. It may appear that way with all the screaming fans. Actually, she's a novelist...
...a very special novelist, and this is a book reading. It's been said Joanne Kathleen Rowling is one of the greatest children's writers in the world, helping to reignite an interest in kids to start reading again.
AS THE AUTHOR OF THE HARRY POTTER SERIES, SHE HAS CAPTURED THE IMAGINATION OF PEOPLE ALL OVER THE WORLD.
OH, BY THE WAY, MY NAME IS ADAM. I'M JUST HERE FOR THE RIDE... SO TO SPEAK... TO SHOW YOU HOW IT ALL HAPPENED.
SO, HOW DID A SHY GIRL FROM ENGLAND END UP HERE?
WELL, IT ALL STARTED NOT SO LONG AGO...

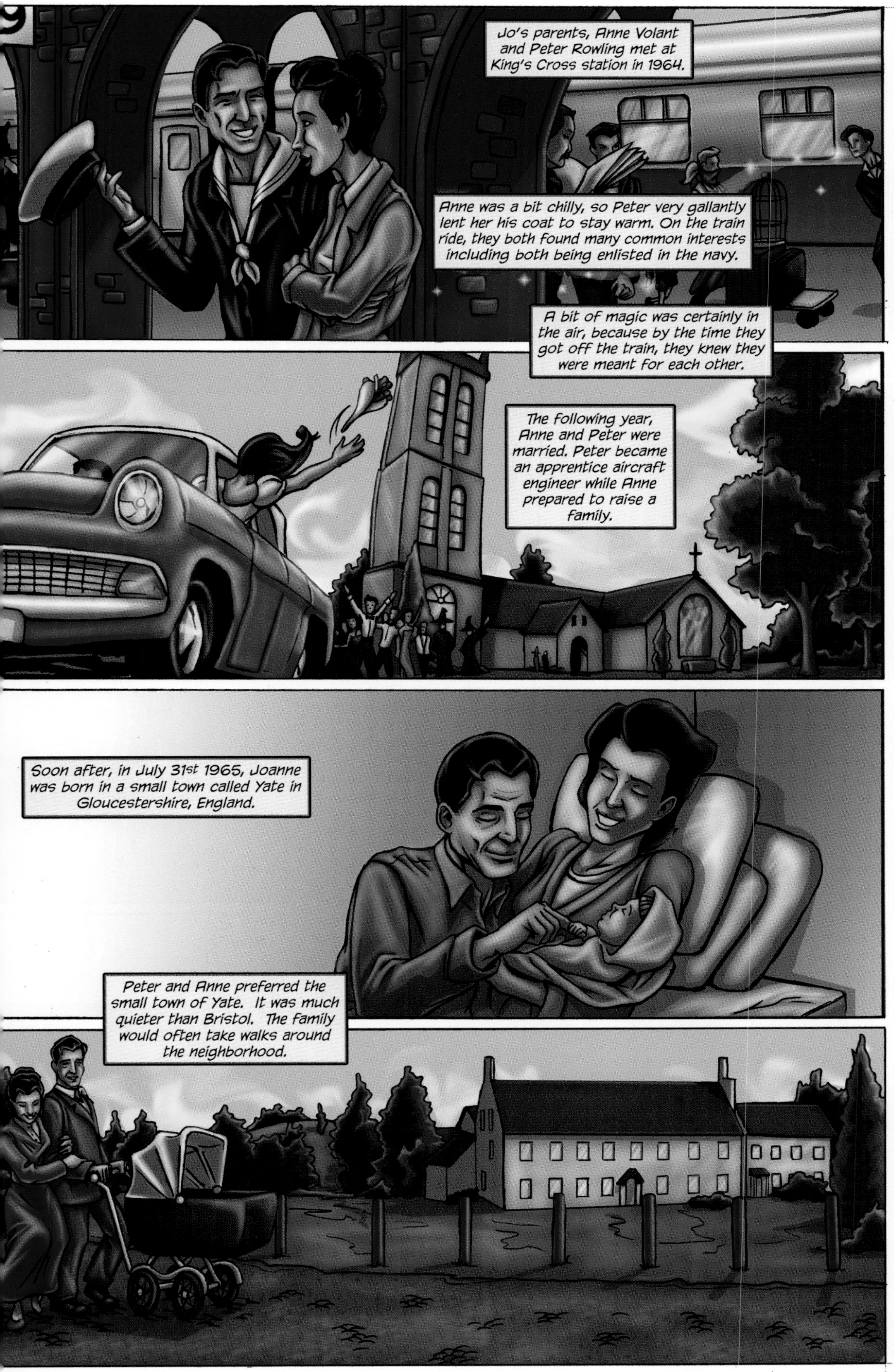
Jo's parents, Anne Volant and Peter Rowling met at King's Cross station in 1964.
Anne was a bit chilly, so Peter very gallantly lent her his coat to stay warm. On the train ride, they both found many common interests including both being enlisted in the navy.
A bit of magic was certainly in the air, because by the time they got off the train, they knew they were meant for each other.
The following year, Anne and Peter were married. Peter became an apprentice aircraft engineer while Anne prepared to raise a family.
Soon after, in July 31st 1965, Joanne was born in a small town called Yate in Gloucestershire, England.
Peter and Anne preferred the small town of Yate. It was much quieter than Bristol. The family would often take walks around the neighborhood.

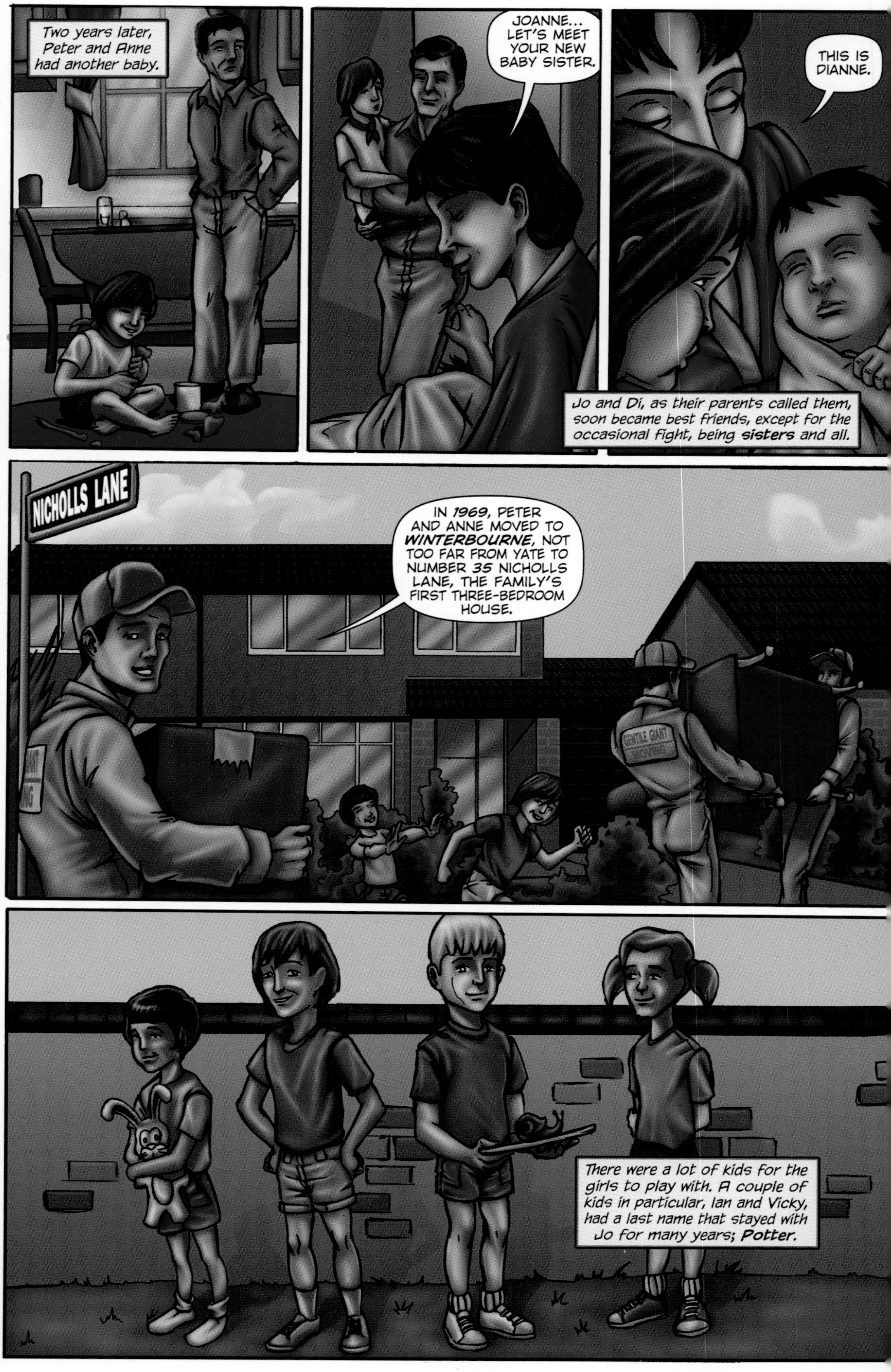

Two years later, Peter and Anne had another baby.
JOANNE... LET'S MEET YOUR NEW BABY SISTER.
THIS IS DIANNE.
Jo and Di, as their parents called them, soon became best friends, except for the occasional fight, being sisters and all.
NICHOLLS LANE
IN 1969, PETER AND ANNE MOVED TO WINTERBOURNE, NOT TOO FAR FROM YATE TO NUMBER 35 NICHOLLS LANE, THE FAMILY'S FIRST THREE-BEDROOM HOUSE.
GENTLE GIANT MOVING
There were a lot of kids for the girls to play with. A couple of kids in particular, Ian and Vicky, had a last name that stayed with Jo for many years; Potter.

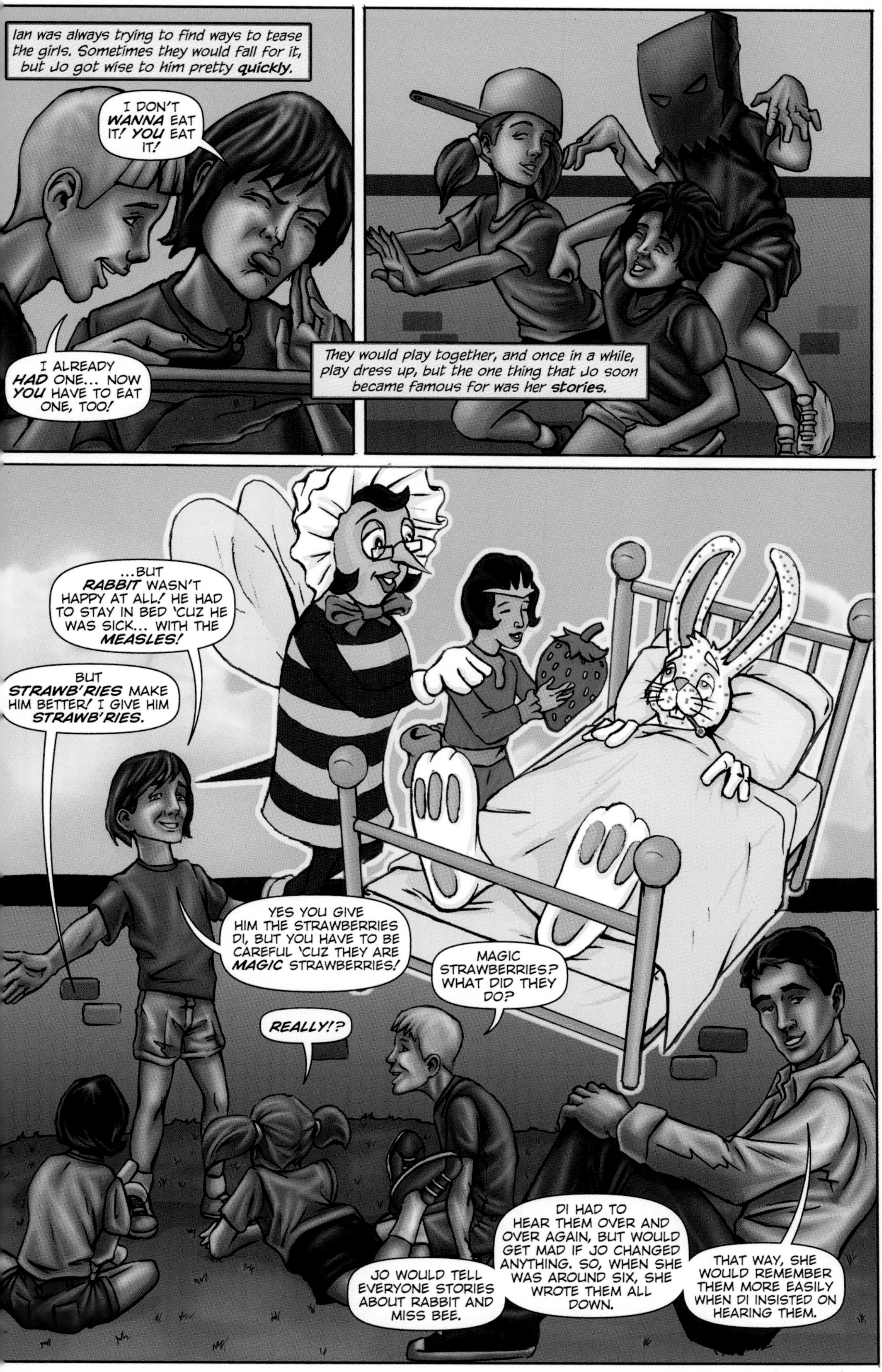

Ian was always trying to find ways to tease the girls. Sometimes they would fall for it, but Jo got wise to him pretty **quickly.**
I DON'T **WANNA** EAT IT! **YOU** EAT IT!
I ALREADY **HAD** ONE... NOW **YOU** HAVE TO EAT ONE, TOO!
They would play together, and once in a while, play dress up, but the one thing that Jo soon became famous for was her **stories.**
...BUT **RABBIT** WASN'T HAPPY AT ALL! HE HAD TO STAY IN BED 'CUZ HE WAS SICK... WITH THE **MEASLES!**
BUT **STRAWB'RIES** MAKE HIM BETTER! I GIVE HIM **STRAWB'RIES.**
YES YOU GIVE HIM THE STRAWBERRIES DI, BUT YOU HAVE TO BE CAREFUL 'CUZ THEY ARE **MAGIC** STRAWBERRIES!
MAGIC STRAWBERRIES? WHAT DID THEY DO?
REALLY!?
JO WOULD TELL EVERYONE STORIES ABOUT RABBIT AND MISS BEE.
DI HAD TO HEAR THEM OVER AND OVER AGAIN, BUT WOULD GET MAD IF JO CHANGED ANYTHING. SO, WHEN SHE WAS AROUND SIX, SHE WROTE THEM ALL DOWN.
THAT WAY, SHE WOULD REMEMBER THEM MORE EASILY WHEN DI INSISTED ON HEARING THEM.

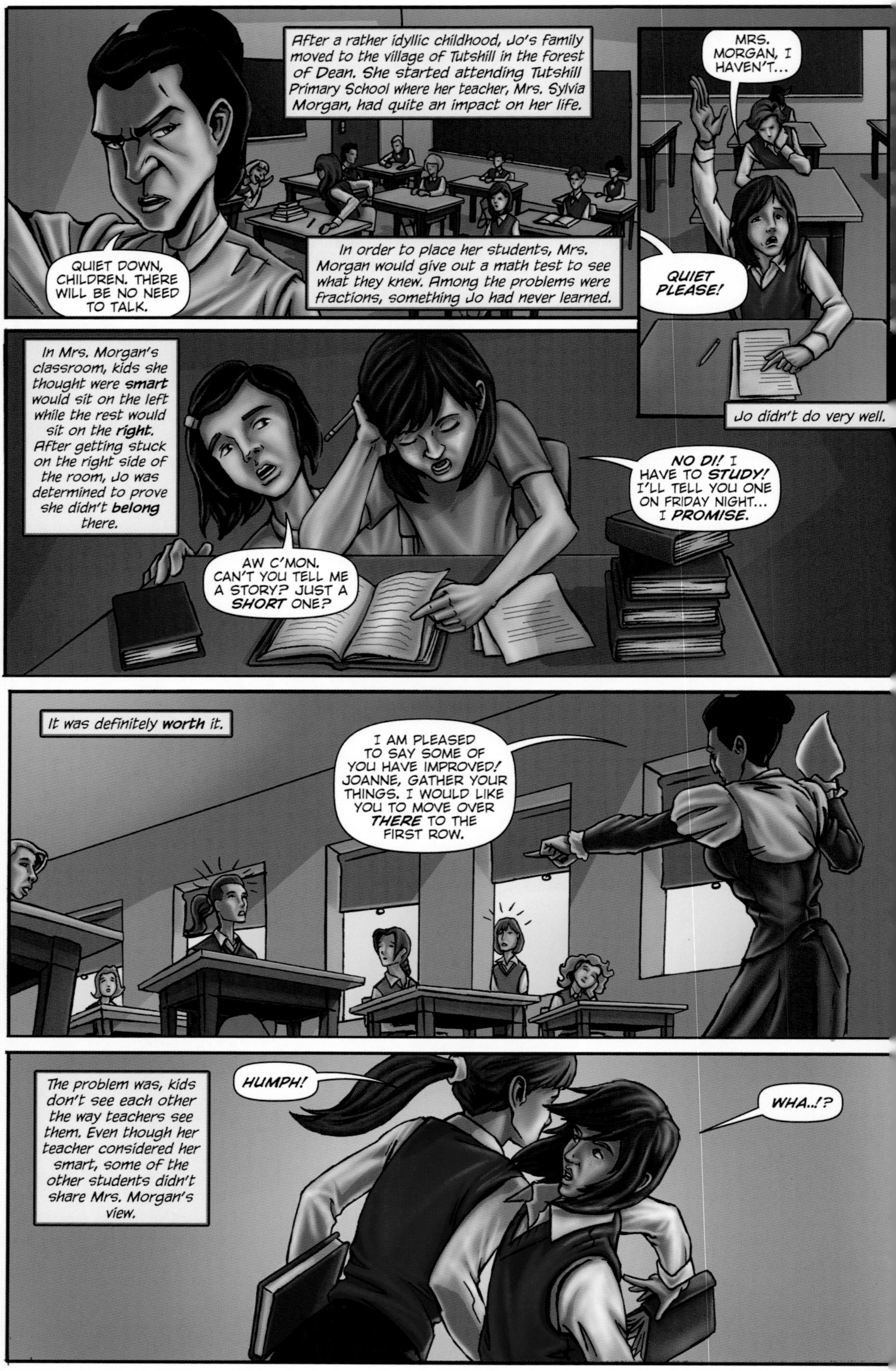

After a rather idyllic childhood, Jo's family moved to the village of Tutshill in the forest of Dean. She started attending Tutshill Primary School where her teacher, Mrs. Sylvia Morgan, had quite an impact on her life.
QUIET DOWN, CHILDREN. THERE WILL BE NO NEED TO TALK.
In order to place her students, Mrs. Morgan would give out a math test to see what they knew. Among the problems were fractions, something Jo had never learned.
MRS. MORGAN, I HAVEN'T...
QUIET PLEASE!
Jo didn't do very well.
In Mrs. Morgan's classroom, kids she thought were smart would sit on the left while the rest would sit on the right. After getting stuck on the right side of the room, Jo was determined to prove she didn't belong there.
AW C'MON. CAN'T YOU TELL ME A STORY? JUST A SHORT ONE?
NO DI! I HAVE TO STUDY! I'LL TELL YOU ONE ON FRIDAY NIGHT... I PROMISE.
It was definitely worth it.
I AM PLEASED TO SAY SOME OF YOU HAVE IMPROVED! JOANNE, GATHER YOUR THINGS. I WOULD LIKE YOU TO MOVE OVER THERE TO THE FIRST ROW.
The problem was, kids don't see each other the way teachers see them. Even though her teacher considered her smart, some of the other students didn't share Mrs. Morgan's view.
HUMPH!
WHA..!?

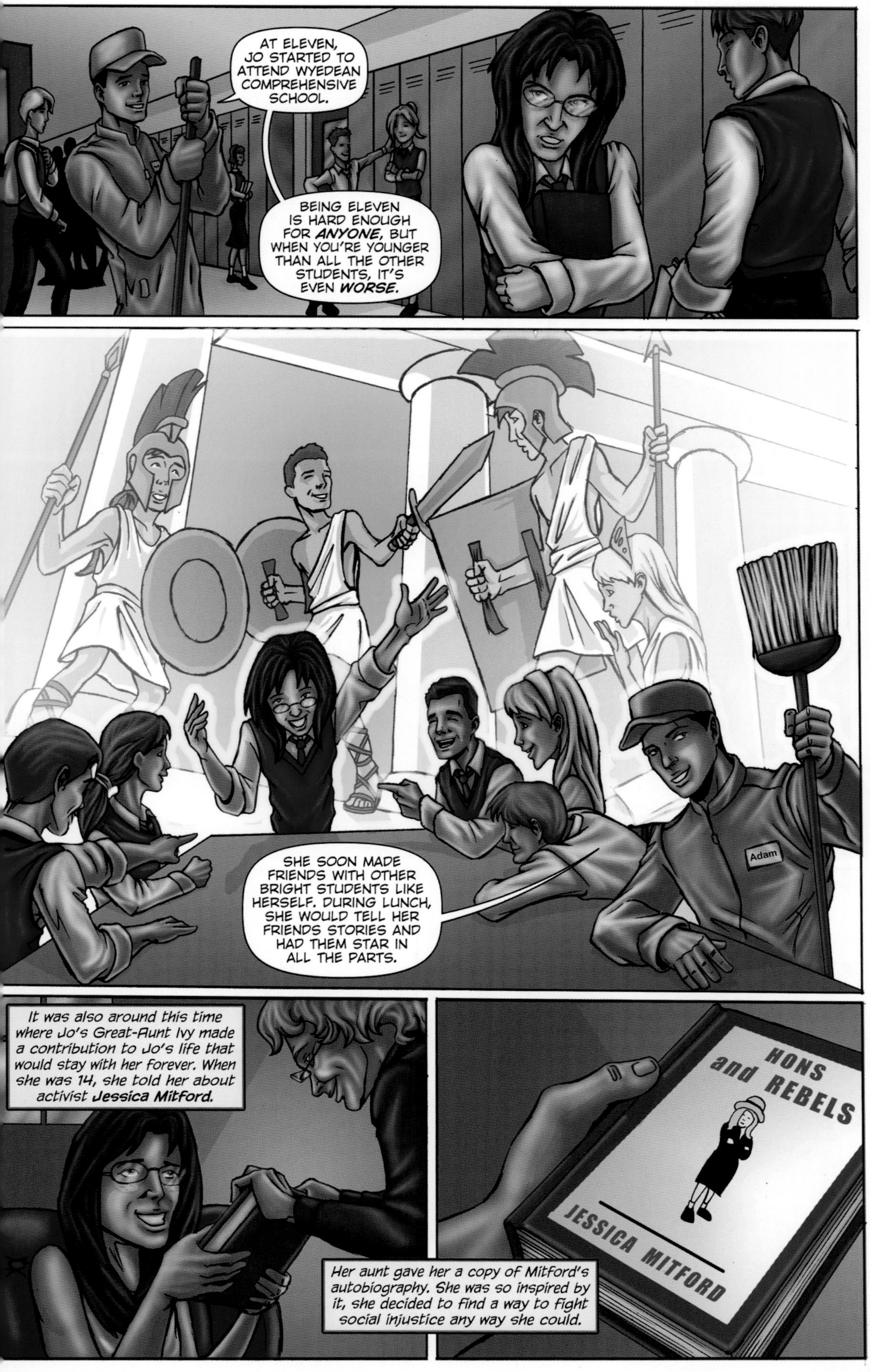
AT ELEVEN, JO STARTED TO ATTEND WYEDEAN COMPREHENSIVE SCHOOL.
BEING ELEVEN IS HARD ENOUGH FOR ANYONE, BUT WHEN YOU'RE YOUNGER THAN ALL THE OTHER STUDENTS, IT'S EVEN WORSE.
Adam
SHE SOON MADE FRIENDS WITH OTHER BRIGHT STUDENTS LIKE HERSELF. DURING LUNCH, SHE WOULD TELL HER FRIENDS STORIES AND HAD THEM STAR IN ALL THE PARTS.
It was also around this time where Jo's Great-Aunt Ivy made a contribution to Jo's life that would stay with her forever. When she was 14, she told her about activist Jessica Mitford.
HONS and REBELS
JESSICA MITFORD
Her aunt gave her a copy of Mitford's autobiography. She was so inspired by it, she decided to find a way to fight social injustice any way she could.

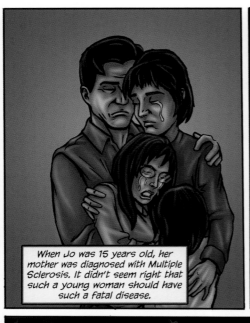

When Jo was 15 years old, her mother was diagnosed with Multiple Sclerosis. It didn't seem right that such a young woman should have such a fatal disease.

OH COME ON, JO, YOU *LIKE* THE SMITHS! A CONCERT IS JUST WHAT YOU *NEED!*

Despite going through such a rough time, Jo's best friend, Sean Harris, was a ray of light. He owned a Ford Anglia and would take Jo and a few others out from time to time.

Sean's friendship had a lasting impression on her life. Later, she would dedicate her second book to him calling him a "getaway driver and a foul-weather friend".

In 1983, Jo graduated from Wyedean. She proved herself academically and became Head Girl in her last year.

CONGRATULATIONS, MISS ROWLING.

JO, WE'RE JUST THINKING ABOUT YOUR *FUTURE.* WE'RE PART OF *EUROPE!* THERE'S ALWAYS GOING TO BE A NICHE FOR BILINGUAL *SECRETARIES!*

I DON'T *KNOW*, DAD...

IT'S WORTH *THINKING* ABOUT.

Most kids take a year off before starting college, but Jo's parents wanted her to have some stability as an adult, suggesting she become an international secretary.

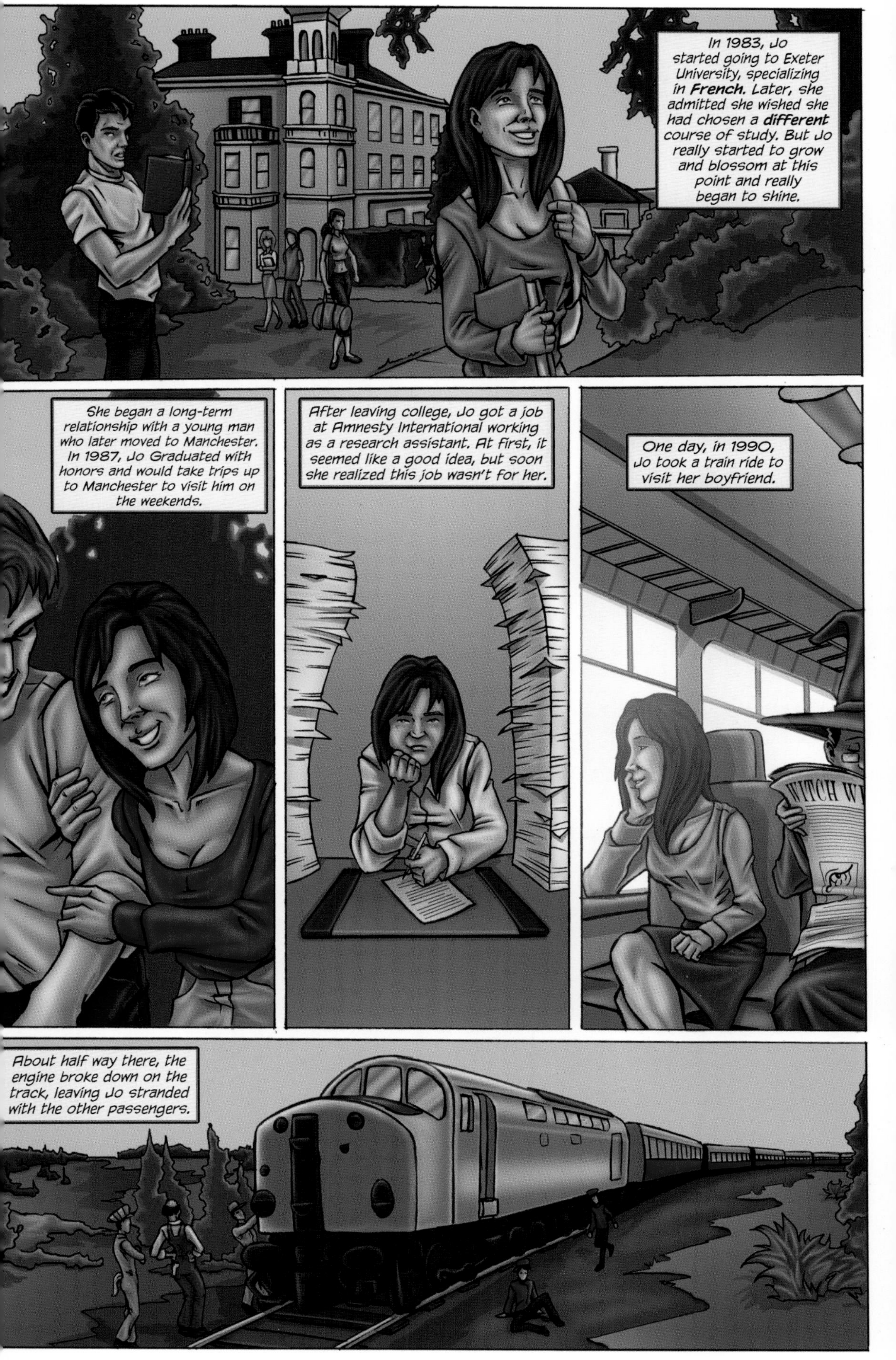
In 1983, Jo started going to Exeter University, specializing in **French**. Later, she admitted she wished she had chosen a ***different*** course of study. But Jo really started to grow and blossom at this point and really began to shine.
She began a long-term relationship with a young man who later moved to Manchester. In 1987, Jo Graduated with honors and would take trips up to Manchester to visit him on the weekends.
After leaving college, Jo got a job at Amnesty International working as a research assistant. At first, it seemed like a good idea, but soon she realized this job wasn't for her.
One day, in 1990, Jo took a train ride to visit her boyfriend.
About half way there, the engine broke down on the track, leaving Jo stranded with the other passengers.

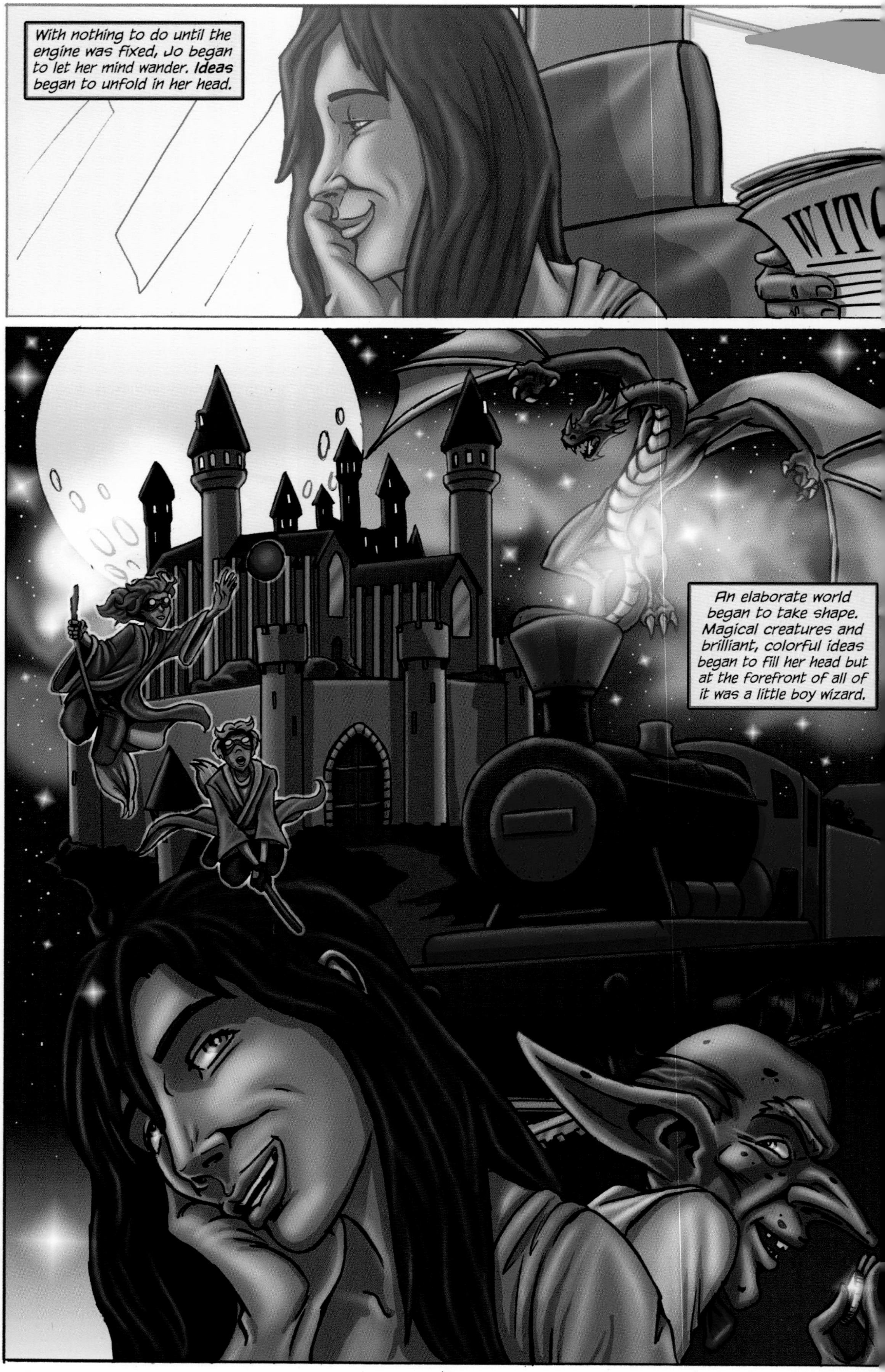
With nothing to do until the engine was fixed, Jo began to let her mind wander. **Ideas** began to unfold in her head.
An elaborate world began to take shape. Magical creatures and brilliant, colorful ideas began to fill her head but at the forefront of all of it was a little boy wizard.

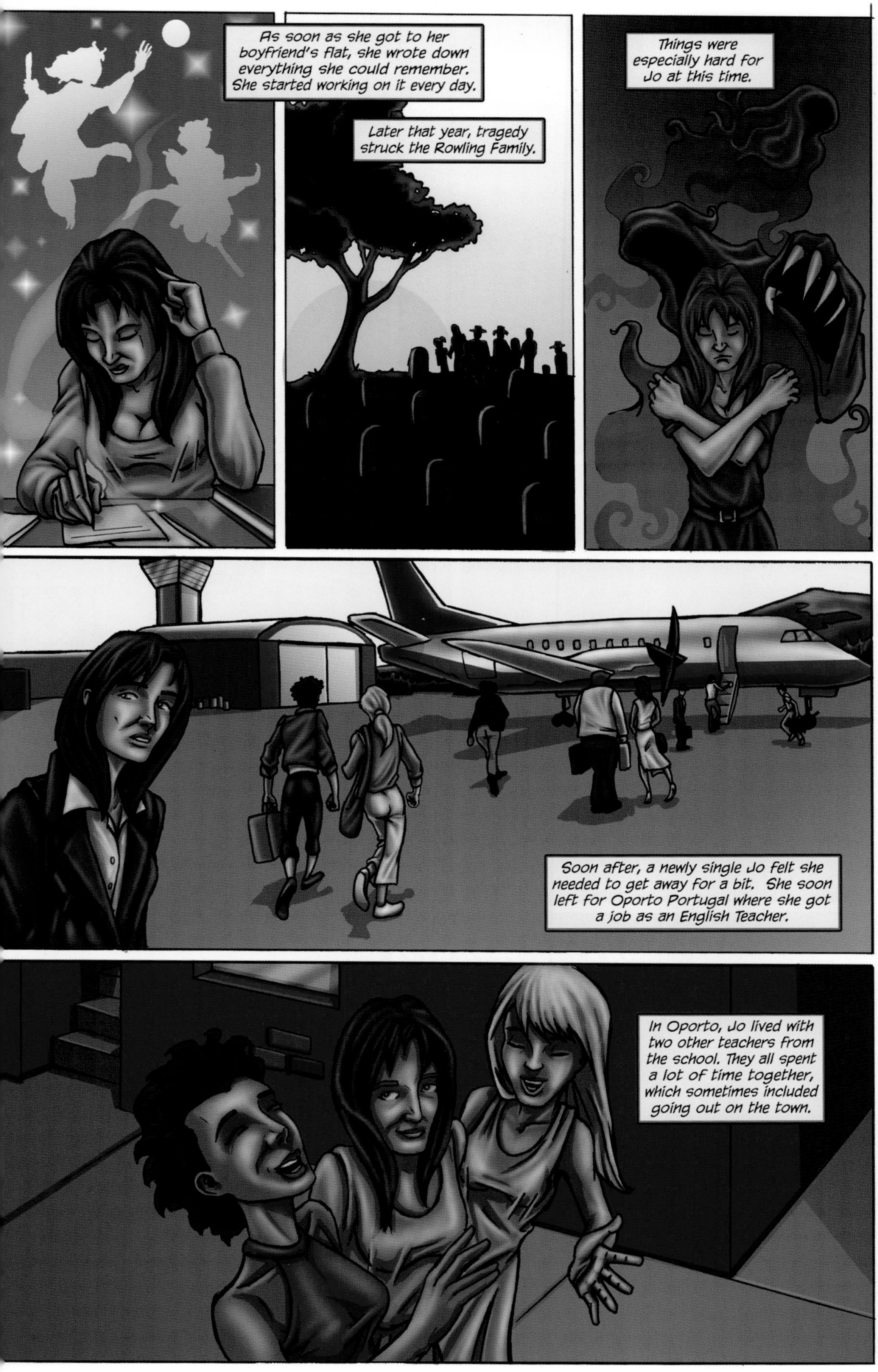
As soon as she got to her boyfriend's flat, she wrote down everything she could remember. She started working on it every day.
Later that year, tragedy struck the Rowling Family.
Things were especially hard for Jo at this time.
Soon after, a newly single Jo felt she needed to get away for a bit. She soon left for Oporto Portugal where she got a job as an English Teacher.
In Oporto, Jo lived with two other teachers from the school. They all spent a lot of time together, which sometimes included going out on the town.

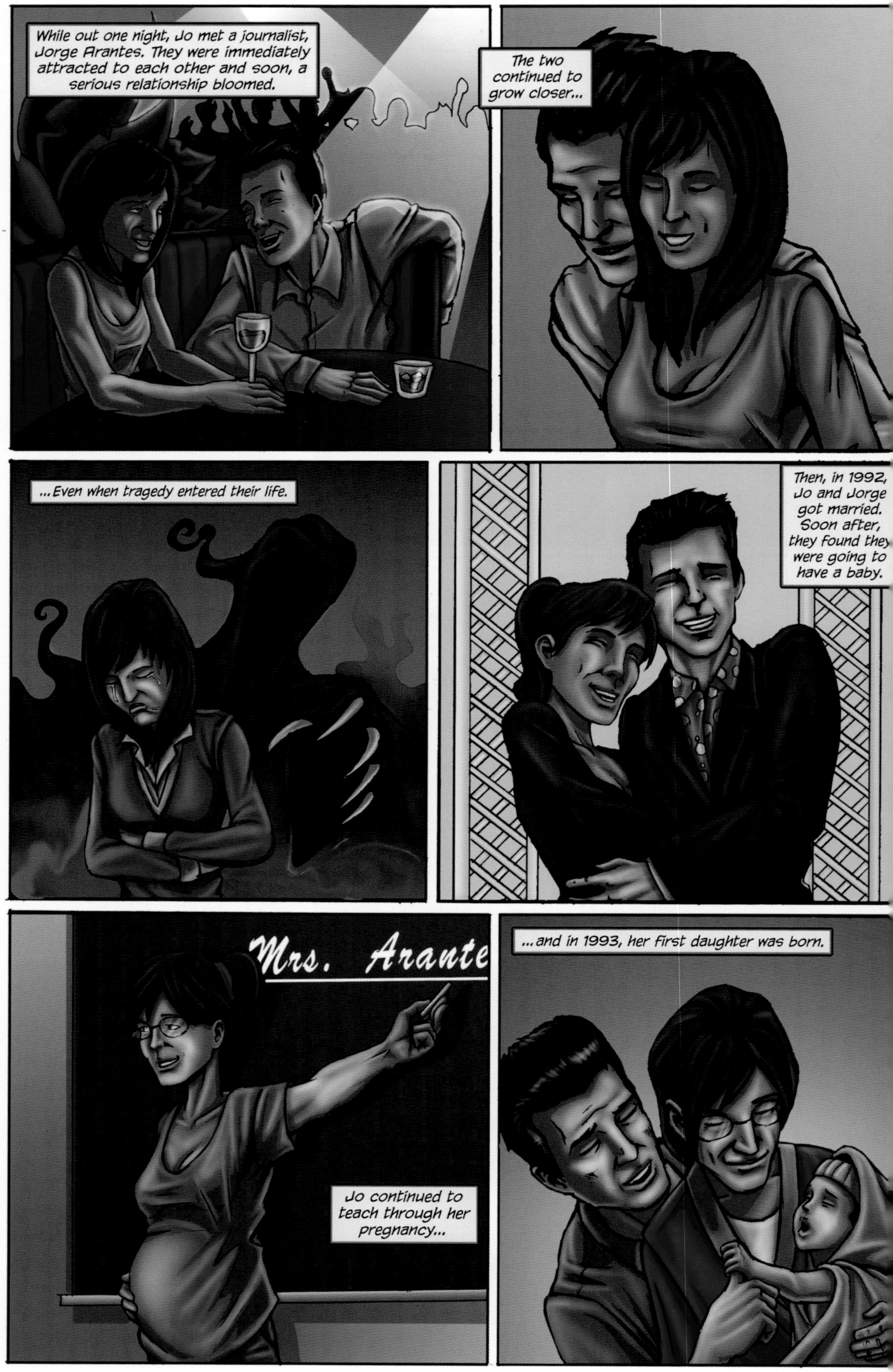
While out one night, Jo met a journalist, Jorge Arantes. They were immediately attracted to each other and soon, a serious relationship bloomed.
The two continued to grow closer...
...Even when tragedy entered their life.
Then, in 1992, Jo and Jorge got married. Soon after, they found they were going to have a baby.
Mrs. Arante
Jo continued to teach through her pregnancy...
...and in 1993, her first daughter was born.

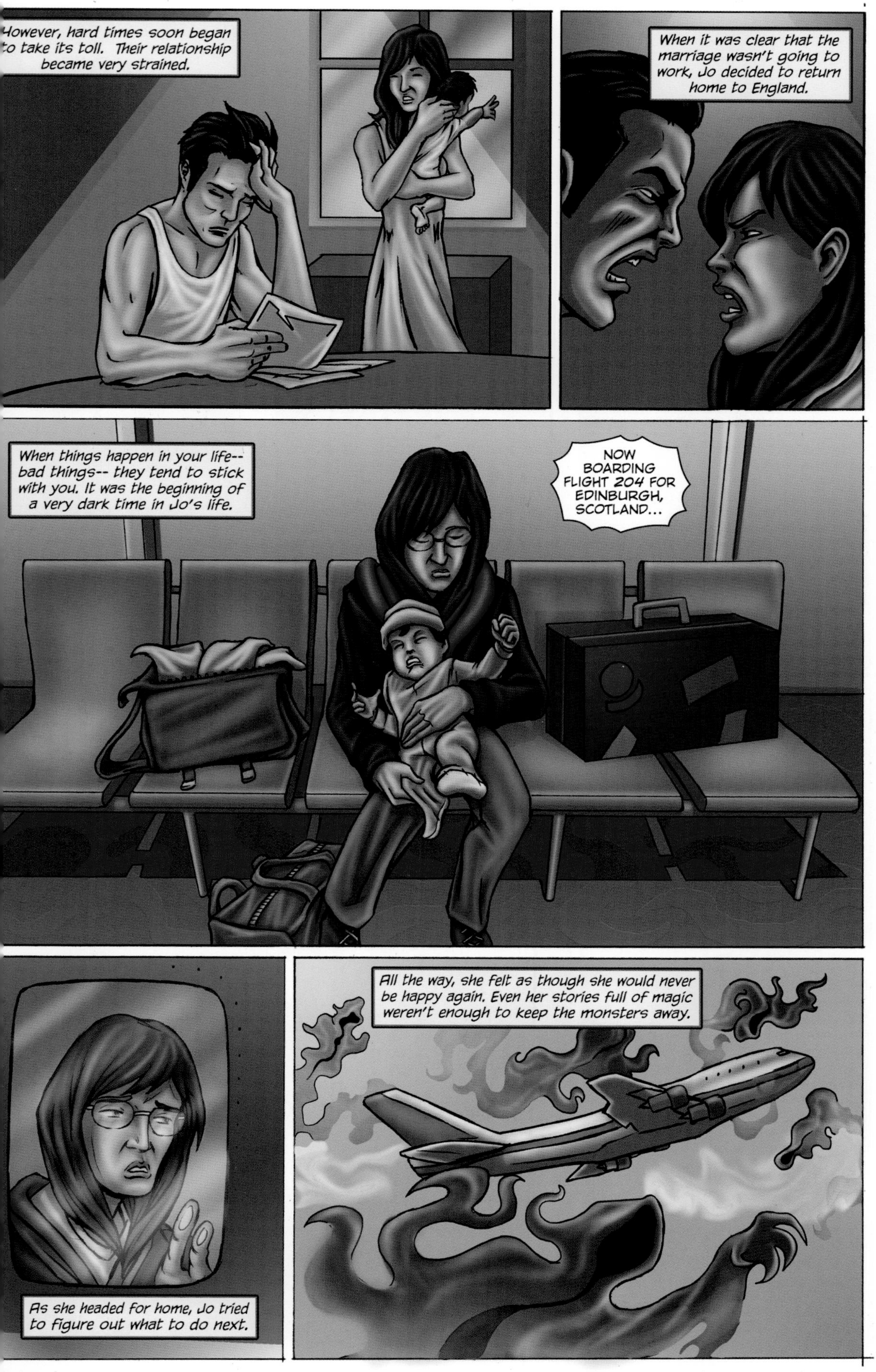
However, hard times soon began to take its toll. Their relationship became very strained.
When it was clear that the marriage wasn't going to work, Jo decided to return home to England.
When things happen in your life-- bad things-- they tend to stick with you. It was the beginning of a very dark time in Jo's life.
NOW BOARDING FLIGHT 204 FOR EDINBURGH, SCOTLAND...
As she headed for home, Jo tried to figure out what to do next.
All the way, she felt as though she would never be happy again. Even her stories full of magic weren't enough to keep the monsters away.

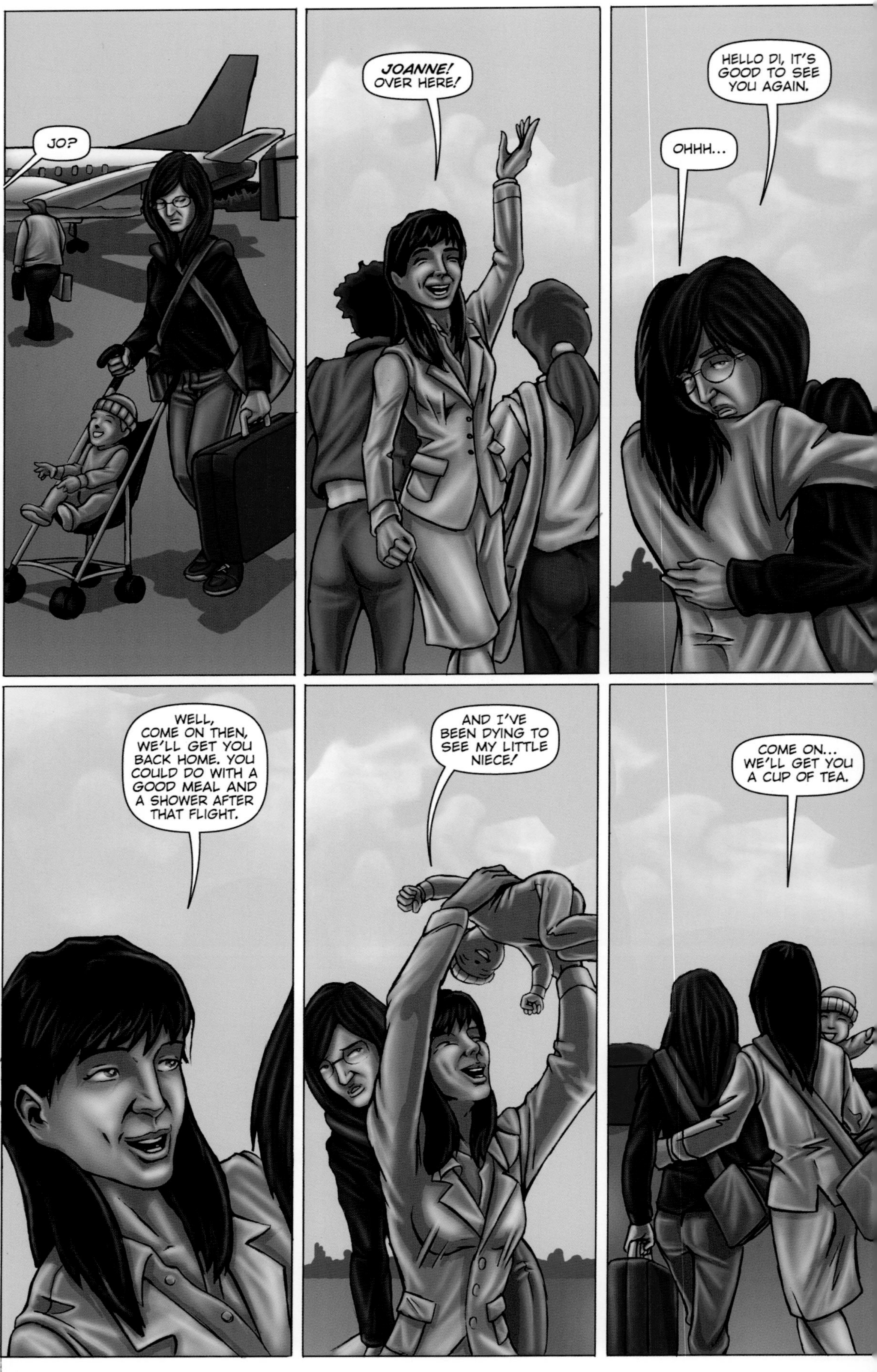
JO?
JOANNE! OVER HERE!
OHHH...
HELLO DI, IT'S GOOD TO SEE YOU AGAIN.
WELL, COME ON THEN, WE'LL GET YOU BACK HOME. YOU COULD DO WITH A GOOD MEAL AND A SHOWER AFTER THAT FLIGHT.
AND I'VE BEEN DYING TO SEE MY LITTLE NIECE!
COME ON... WE'LL GET YOU A CUP OF TEA.

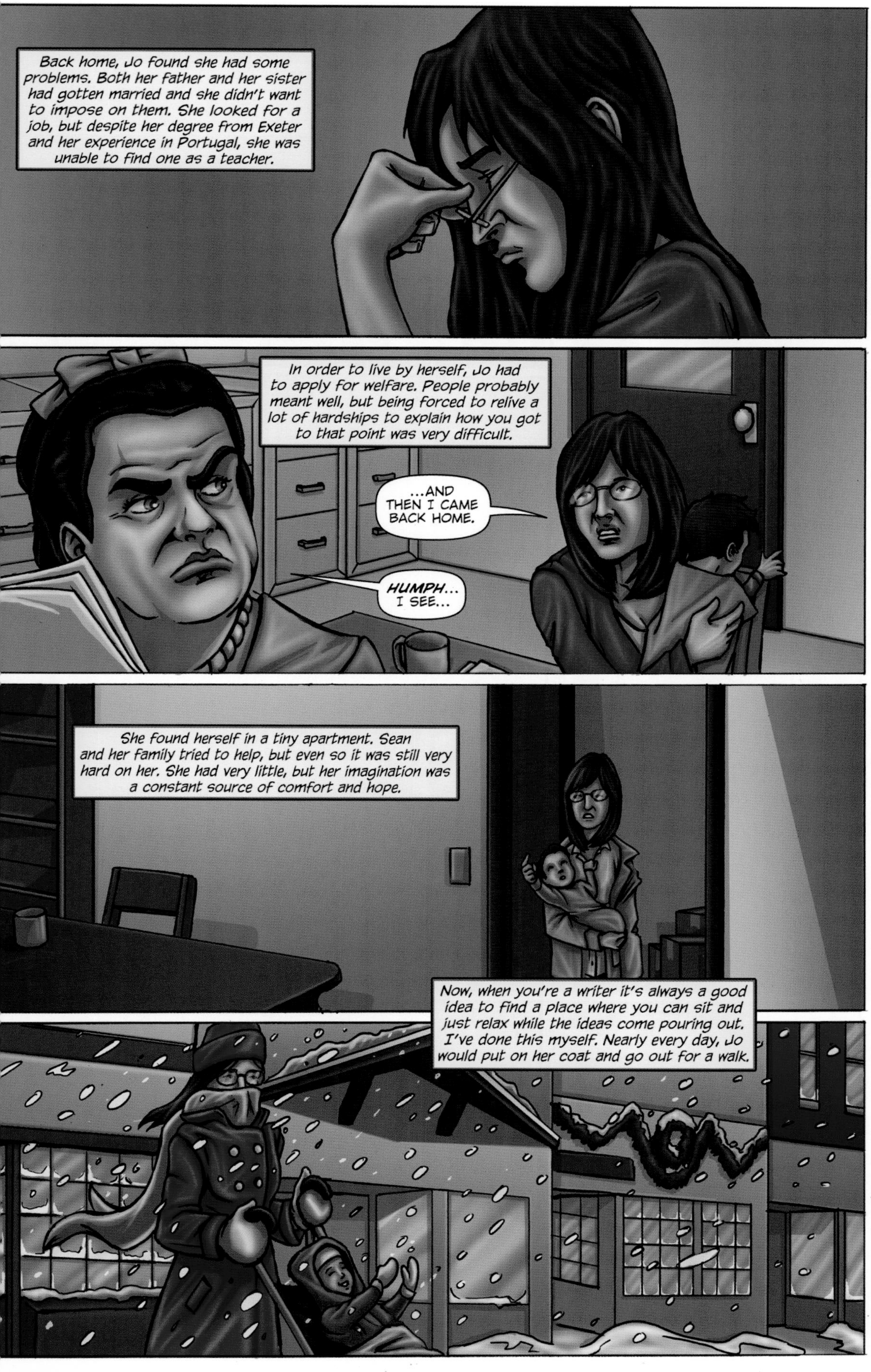

Back home, Jo found she had some problems. Both her father and her sister had gotten married and she didn't want to impose on them. She looked for a job, but despite her degree from Exeter and her experience in Portugal, she was unable to find one as a teacher.
In order to live by herself, Jo had to apply for welfare. People probably meant well, but being forced to relive a lot of hardships to explain how you got to that point was very difficult.
...AND THEN I CAME BACK HOME.
HUMPH... I SEE...
She found herself in a tiny apartment. Sean and her family tried to help, but even so it was still very hard on her. She had very little, but her imagination was a constant source of comfort and hope.
Now, when you're a writer it's always a good idea to find a place where you can sit and just relax while the ideas come pouring out. I've done this myself. Nearly every day, Jo would put on her coat and go out for a walk.

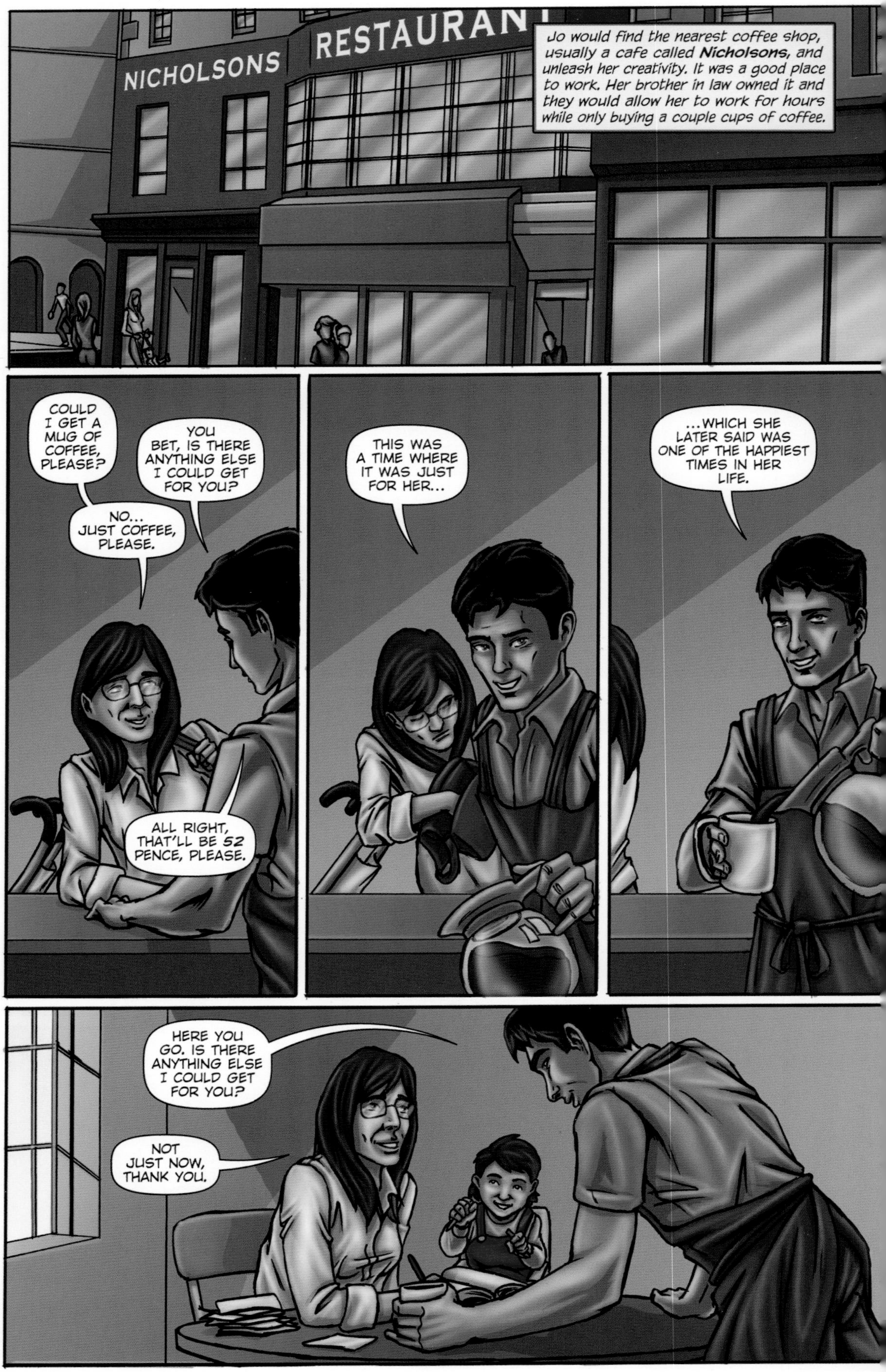
RESTAURANT
NICHOLSONS
Jo would find the nearest coffee shop, usually a cafe called **Nicholsons,** and unleash her creativity. It was a good place to work. Her brother in law owned it and they would allow her to work for hours while only buying a couple cups of coffee.
COULD I GET A MUG OF COFFEE, PLEASE?
YOU BET, IS THERE ANYTHING ELSE I COULD GET FOR YOU?
NO... JUST COFFEE, PLEASE.
ALL RIGHT, THAT'LL BE 52 PENCE, PLEASE.
THIS WAS A TIME WHERE IT WAS JUST FOR HER...
...WHICH SHE LATER SAID WAS ONE OF THE HAPPIEST TIMES IN HER LIFE.
HERE YOU GO. IS THERE ANYTHING ELSE I COULD GET FOR YOU?
NOT JUST NOW, THANK YOU.

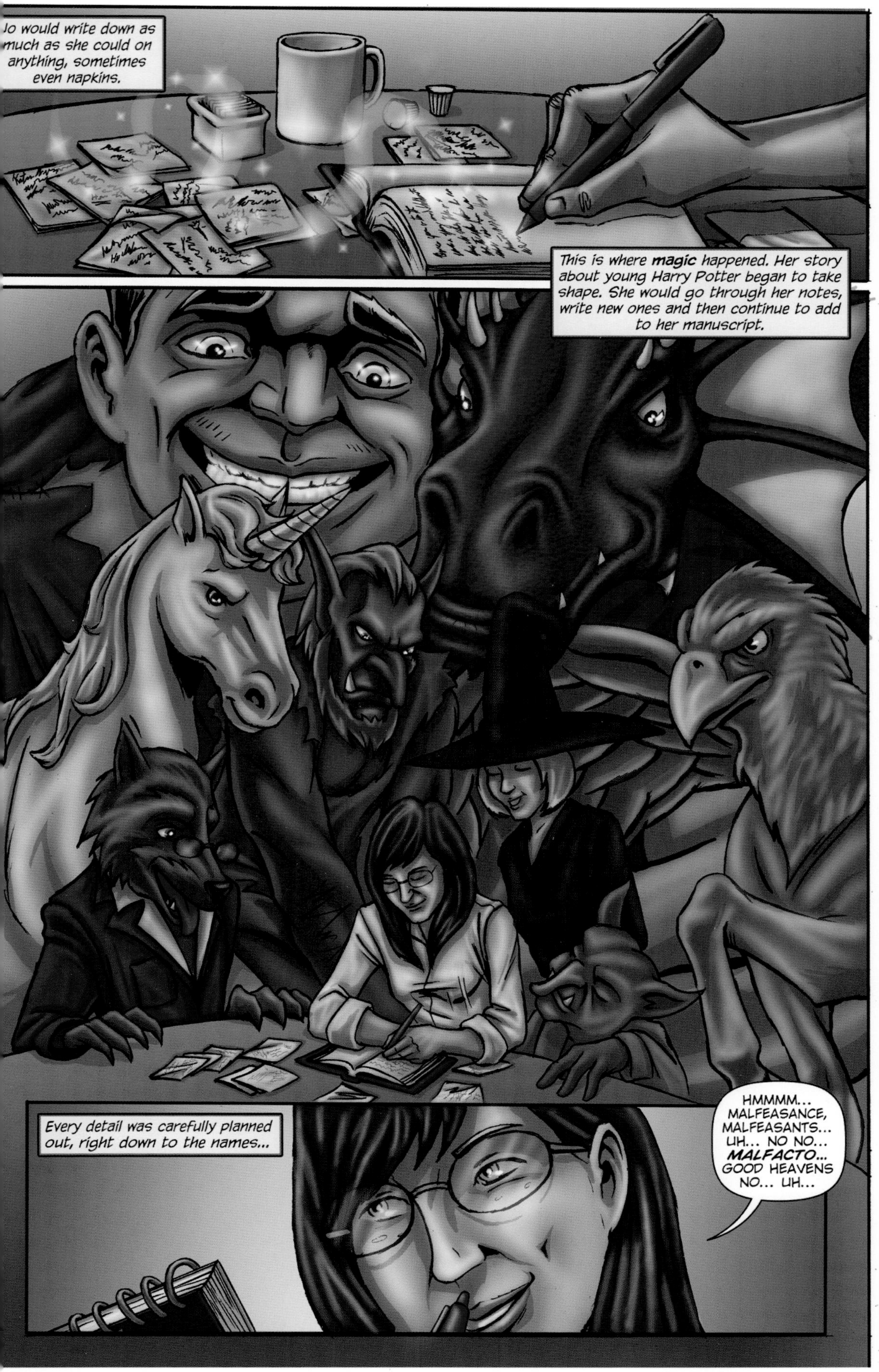

Jo would write down as much as she could on anything, sometimes even napkins.
This is where **magic** happened. Her story about young Harry Potter began to take shape. She would go through her notes, write new ones and then continue to add to her manuscript.
Every detail was carefully planned out, right down to the names...
HMMMM... MALFEASANCE, MALFEASANTS... UH... NO NO... **MALFACTO**... GOOD HEAVENS NO... UH...

Determined to give her daughter a better life. Jo looked for a teaching job. She found she would have to do a course at Moray House teaching school in Edinburgh. Before she started, she wanted to get the story done before school took up her time.

After a **superhuman** effort on her part, Jo finished her first novel, and typed up two copies on a manual typewriter.

HARRY POTTER AND THE PHILOSOPHER'S STONE

BY JOANNE ROWLING

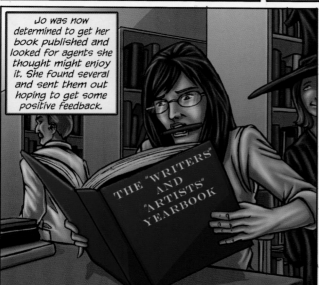

Jo was now determined to get her book published and looked for agents she thought might enjoy it. She found several and sent them out hoping to get some positive feedback.

THE "WRITERS" AND "ARTISTS" YEARBOOK

In the office of Christopher Little, a young and imaginative assistant, Bryony Evens read the first chapter and showed it to her boss right away.

HARRY POTTER AND THE PHILOSOPHER'S STONE

BY JOANNE ROWLING

After he read it, Little took her on as a client! After a few changes, Jo's new agent began sending the book to several publishers. Then in 1996, a small publisher called **Bloomsbury** decided to accept it and set her up with her first advance.

However, Bloomsbury was worried that a book by a woman wouldn't get **boy** readers so they asked her to use her initials. Jo didn't have a middle initial so she had to come up with one...

WELL... MY GRANDMOTHER'S NAME WAS KATHLEEN. DOES **J.K. ROWLING** WORK?

Before her first book came out, Jo applies for a grant from the **Scottish Arts Council**. Despite never having been published, Jo was considered and awarded a grant to finish the next book. Soon after, *Harry Potter and the Sorcerer's Stone* was published.

*Released in the United States as "**Harry Potter and the Sorcerer's Stone**".

Publishers in the U.S. soon heard about this new superstar writer and began making offers for the book. Scholastic made her the biggest offer any children's author has ever been made.

H-HOW MUCH?

THEY'VE OFFERED TO BUY THE RIGHTS FOR $105,000.

OH MY GOD...

NOW JOANNE, WITH THE SUCCESS OF YOUR FIRST BOOK, PEOPLE ARE GOING TO WANT TO KNOW MORE ABOUT YOU. YOU MIGHT FIND YOUR LIFE BECOMING PUBLIC PROPERTY.

UH... REALLY?

Jo wasn't crazy about the idea of her life becoming so public, but it was all happening so fast. She hoped the rest of her books would measure up.

With her first book a success, Jo felt very worried that the next book wouldn't measure up to everything her readers would hope for. The pressure seemed way too much.

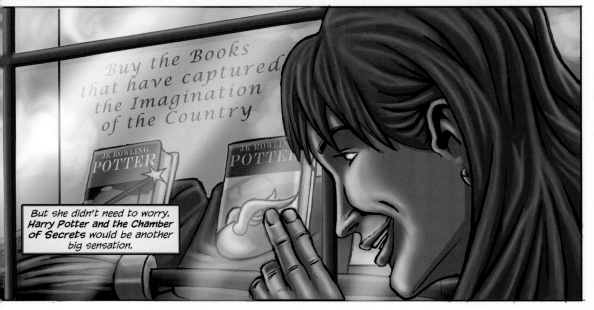

Buy the Books that have captured the Imagination of the Country

JK ROWLING POTTER

JK ROWLING POTTER

But she didn't need to worry. *Harry Potter and the Chamber of Secrets* would be another big sensation.

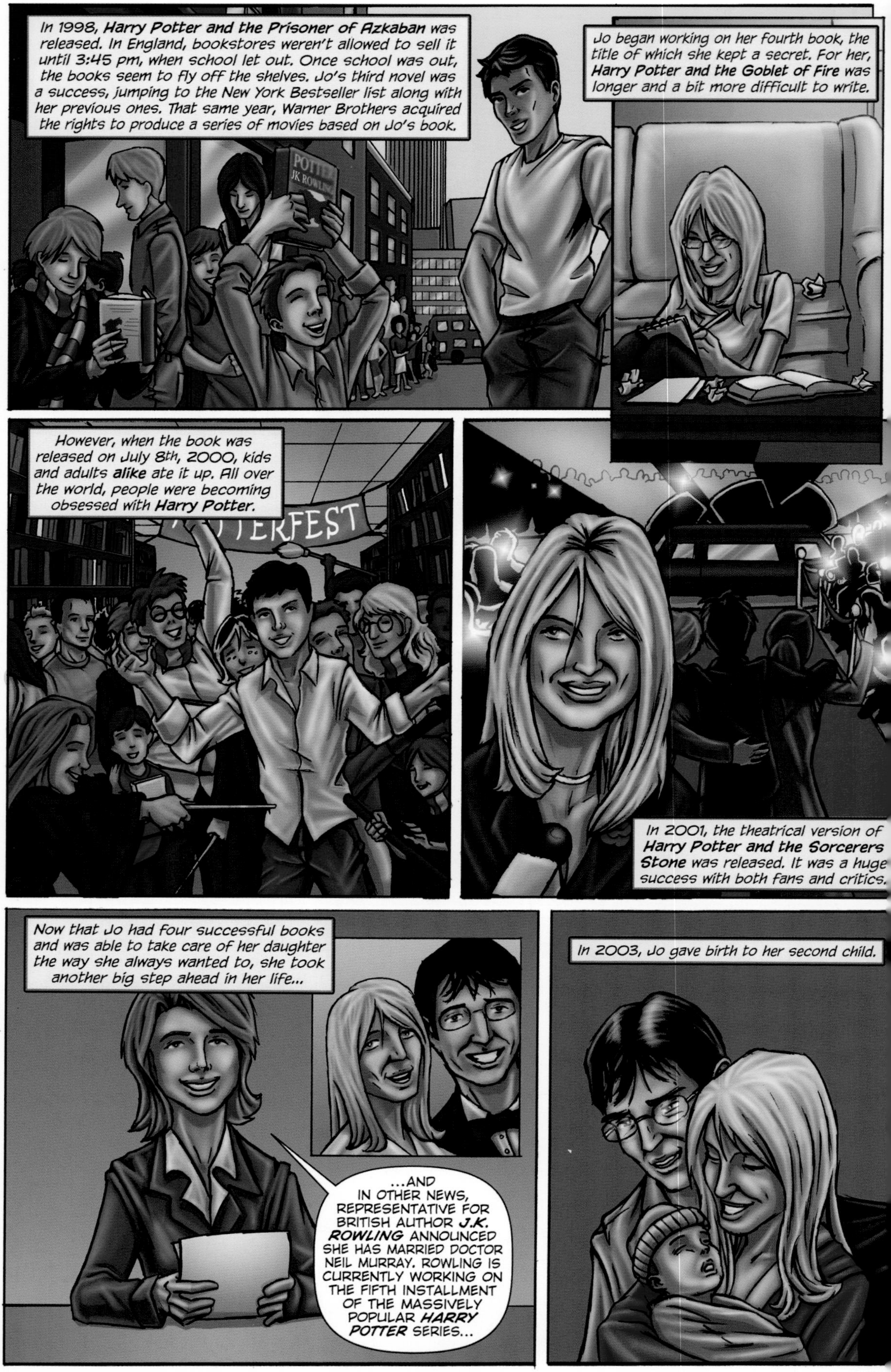
In 1998, Harry Potter and the Prisoner of Azkaban was released. In England, bookstores weren't allowed to sell it until 3:45 pm, when school let out. Once school was out, the books seem to fly off the shelves. Jo's third novel was a success, jumping to the New York Bestseller list along with her previous ones. That same year, Warner Brothers acquired the rights to produce a series of movies based on Jo's book.
POTTER
JK ROWLING
Jo began working on her fourth book, the title of which she kept a secret. For her, Harry Potter and the Goblet of Fire was longer and a bit more difficult to write.
However, when the book was released on July 8th, 2000, kids and adults alike ate it up. All over the world, people were becoming obsessed with Harry Potter.
In 2001, the theatrical version of Harry Potter and the Sorcerers Stone was released. It was a huge success with both fans and critics.
Now that Jo had four successful books and was able to take care of her daughter the way she always wanted to, she took another big step ahead in her life...
...AND IN OTHER NEWS, REPRESENTATIVE FOR BRITISH AUTHOR J.K. ROWLING ANNOUNCED SHE HAS MARRIED DOCTOR NEIL MURRAY. ROWLING IS CURRENTLY WORKING ON THE FIFTH INSTALLMENT OF THE MASSIVELY POPULAR HARRY POTTER SERIES...
In 2003, Jo gave birth to her second child.

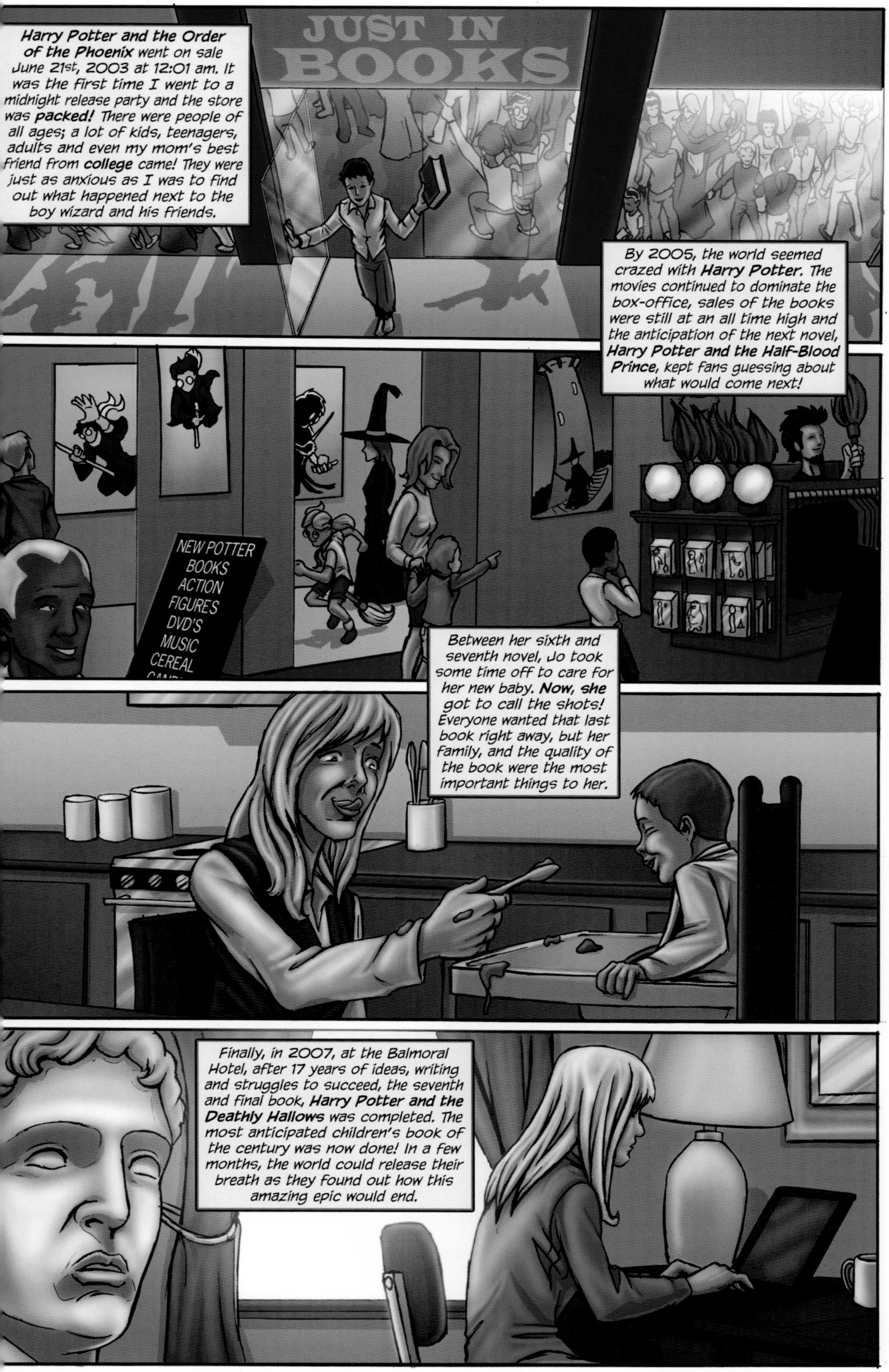
JUST IN
BOOKS
Harry Potter and the Order of the Phoenix went on sale June 21st, 2003 at 12:01 am. It was the first time I went to a midnight release party and the store was packed! There were people of all ages; a lot of kids, teenagers, adults and even my mom's best friend from college came! They were just as anxious as I was to find out what happened next to the boy wizard and his friends.
By 2005, the world seemed crazed with Harry Potter. The movies continued to dominate the box-office, sales of the books were still at an all time high and the anticipation of the next novel, Harry Potter and the Half-Blood Prince, kept fans guessing about what would come next!
NEW POTTER BOOKS ACTION FIGURES DVD'S MUSIC CEREAL
Between her sixth and seventh novel, Jo took some time off to care for her new baby. Now, she got to call the shots! Everyone wanted that last book right away, but her family, and the quality of the book were the most important things to her.
Finally, in 2007, at the Balmoral Hotel, after 17 years of ideas, writing and struggles to succeed, the seventh and final book, Harry Potter and the Deathly Hallows was completed. The most anticipated children's book of the century was now done! In a few months, the world could release their breath as they found out how this amazing epic would end.

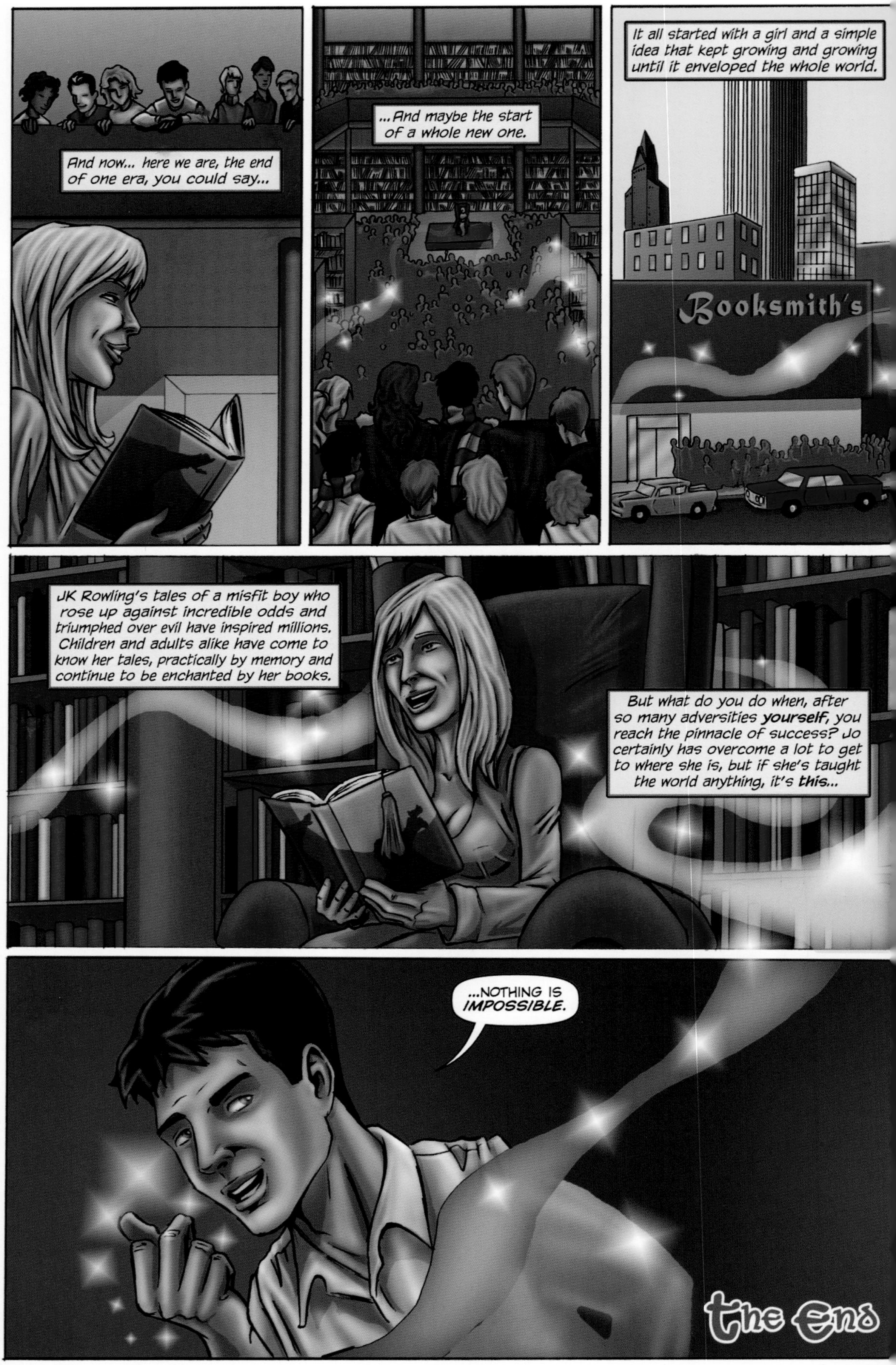
And now... here we are, the end of one era, you could say...
...And maybe the start of a whole new one.
It all started with a girl and a simple idea that kept growing and growing until it enveloped the whole world.
Booksmith's
JK Rowling's tales of a misfit boy who rose up against incredible odds and triumphed over evil have inspired millions. Children and adults alike have come to know her tales, practically by memory and continue to be enchanted by her books.
But what do you do when, after so many adversities **yourself**, you reach the pinnacle of success? Jo certainly has overcome a lot to get to where she is, but if she's taught the world anything, it's **this**...
...NOTHING IS *IMPOSSIBLE*.
The End

A History of Magic

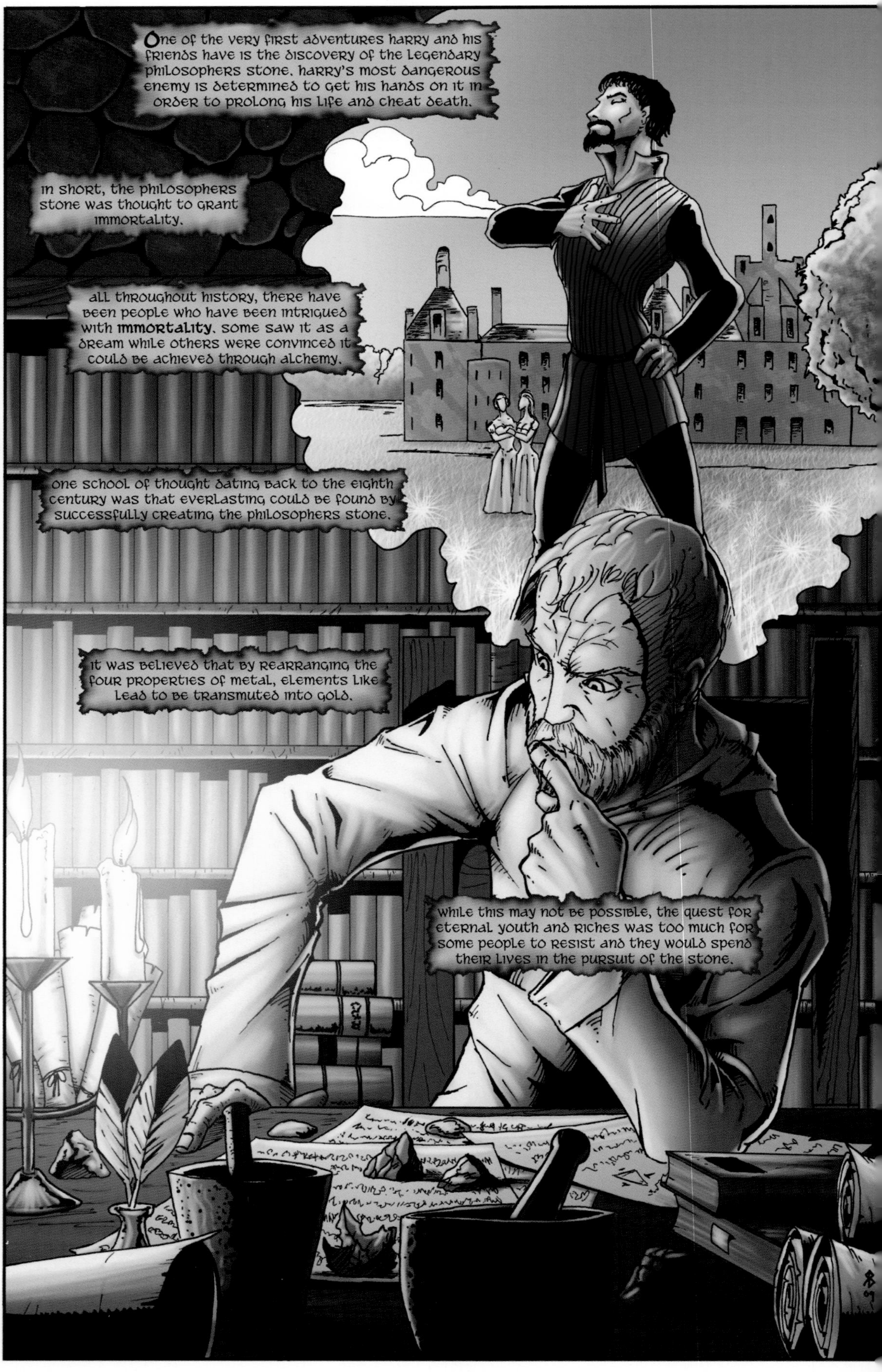
One of the very first adventures harry and his friends have is the discovery of the legendary philosophers stone. harry's most dangerous enemy is determined to get his hands on it in order to prolong his life and cheat death.
in short, the philosophers stone was thought to grant immortality.
all throughout history, there have been people who have been intrigued with immortality. some saw it as a dream while others were convinced it could be achieved through alchemy.
one school of thought dating back to the eighth century was that everlasting could be found by successfully creating the philosophers stone.
it was believed that by rearranging the four properties of metal, elements like lead to be transmuted into gold.
while this may not be possible, the quest for eternal youth and riches was too much for some people to resist and they would spend their lives in the pursuit of the stone.

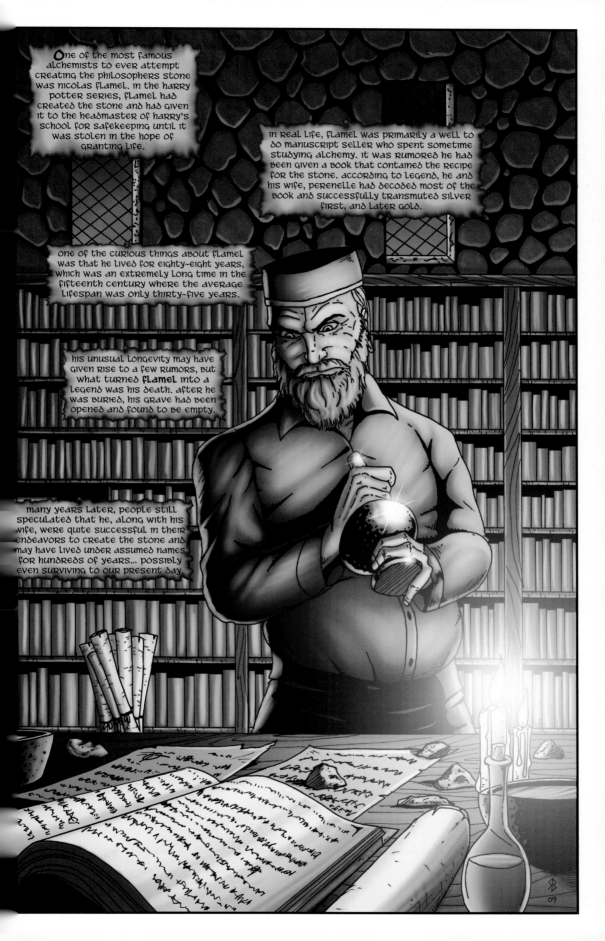

One of the most famous alchemists to ever attempt creating the philosophers stone was nicolas flamel. in the harry potter series, flamel had created the stone and had given it to the headmaster of harry's school for safekeeping until it was stolen in the hope of granting life.

in real life, flamel was primarily a well to do manuscript seller who spent sometime studying alchemy. it was rumored he had been given a book that contained the recipe for the stone. according to legend, he and his wife, perenelle had decoded most of the book and successfully transmuted silver first, and later gold.

one of the curious things about flamel was that he lived for eighty-eight years, which was an extremely long time in the fifteenth century where the average lifespan was only thirty-five years.

his unusual longevity may have given rise to a few rumors, but what turned flamel into a legend was his death. after he was buried, his grave had been opened and found to be empty.

many years later, people still speculated that he, along with his wife, were quite successful in their endeavors to create the stone and may have lived under assumed names, for hundreds of years... possibly even surviving to our present day.

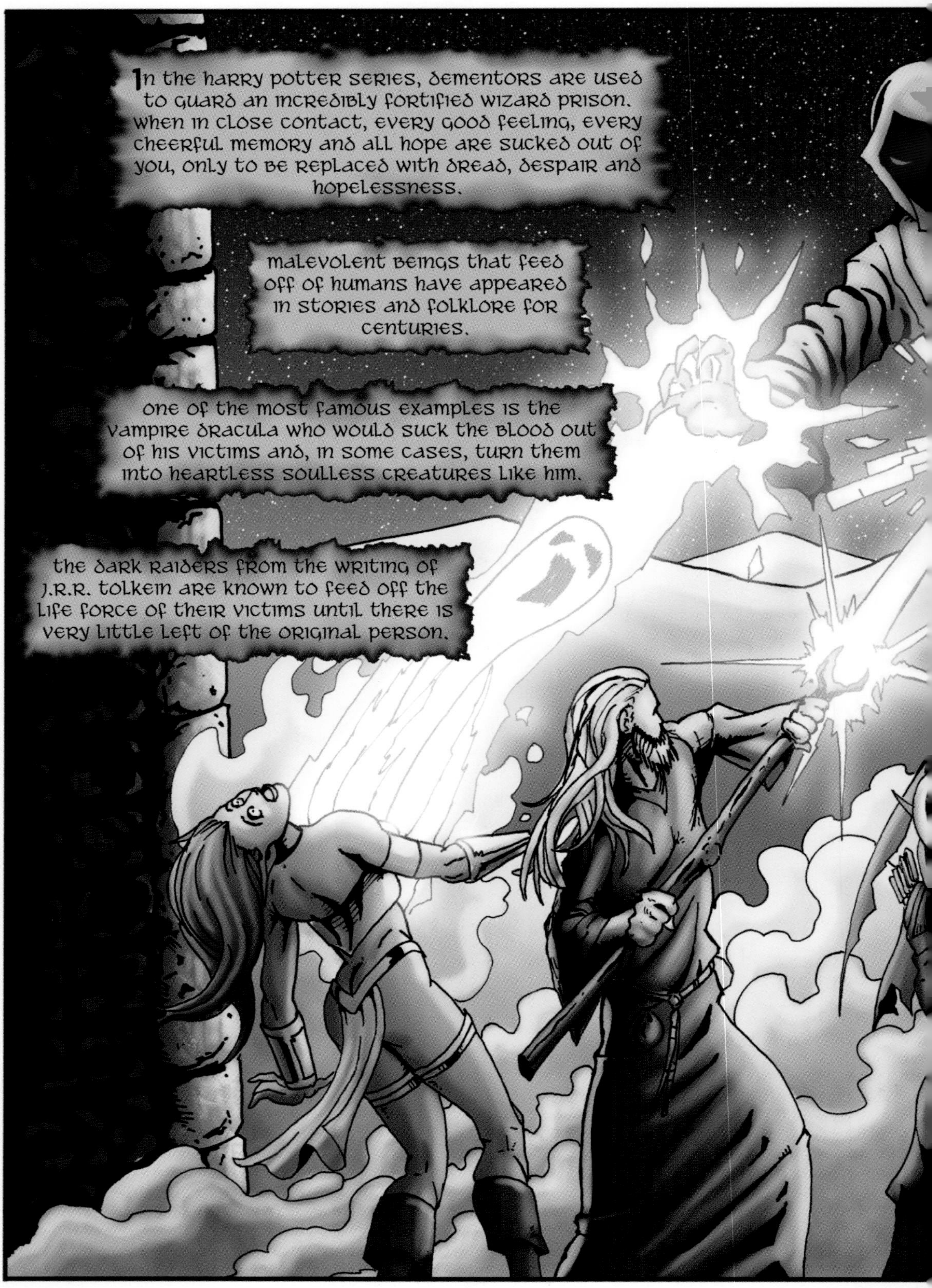
In the harry potter series, dementors are used to guard an incredibly fortified wizard prison. when in close contact, every good feeling, every cheerful memory and all hope are sucked out of you, only to be replaced with dread, despair and hopelessness.
malevolent beings that feed off of humans have appeared in stories and folklore for centuries.
one of the most famous examples is the vampire dracula who would suck the blood out of his victims and, in some cases, turn them into heartless soulless creatures like him.
the dark raiders from the writing of J.R.R. tolkein are known to feed off the life force of their victims until there is very little left of the original person.

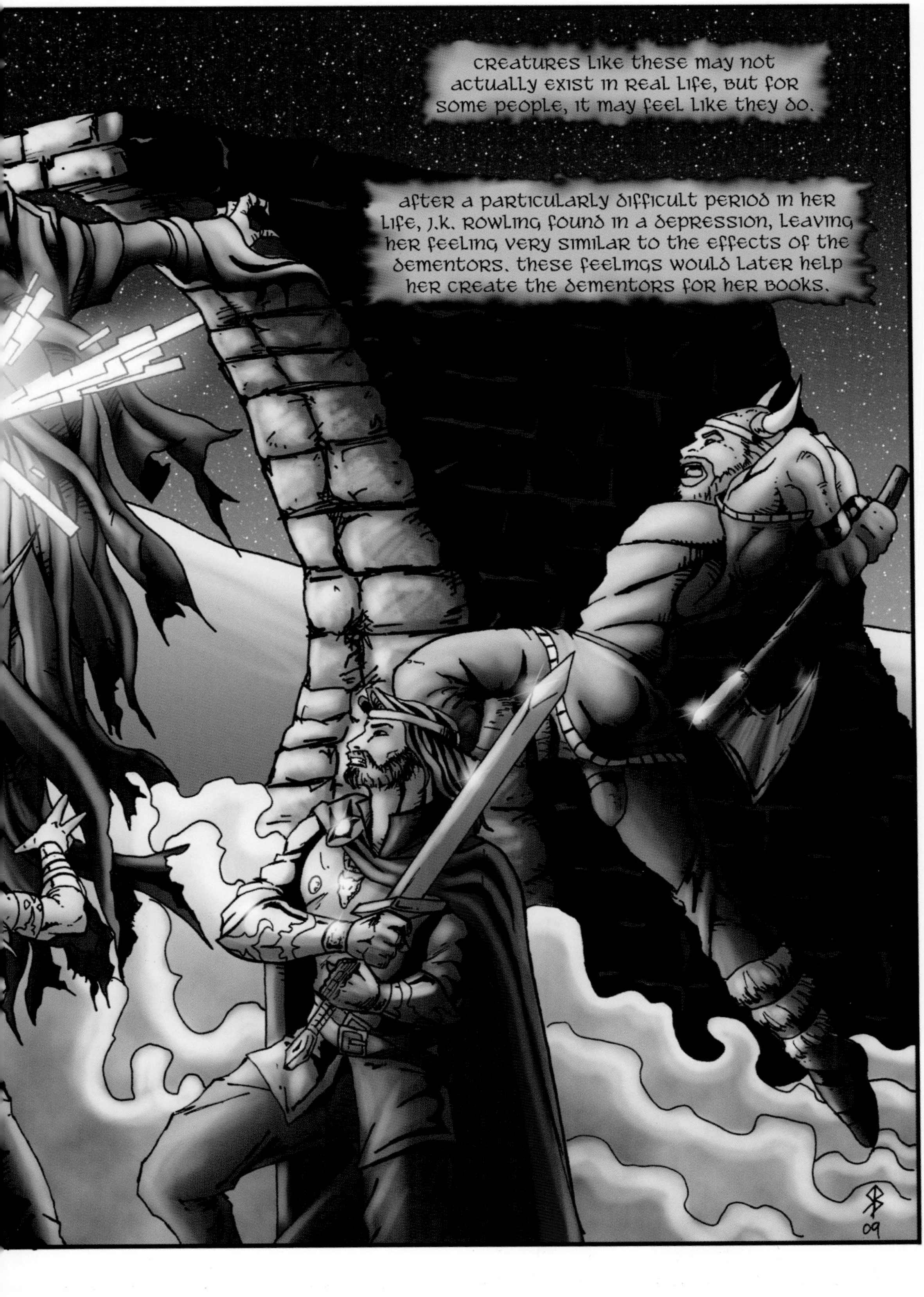

creatures like these may not actually exist in real life, but for some people, it may feel like they do.
after a particularly difficult period in her life, J.K. Rowling found in a depression, leaving her feeling very similar to the effects of the dementors. these feelings would later help her create the dementors for her books.
09

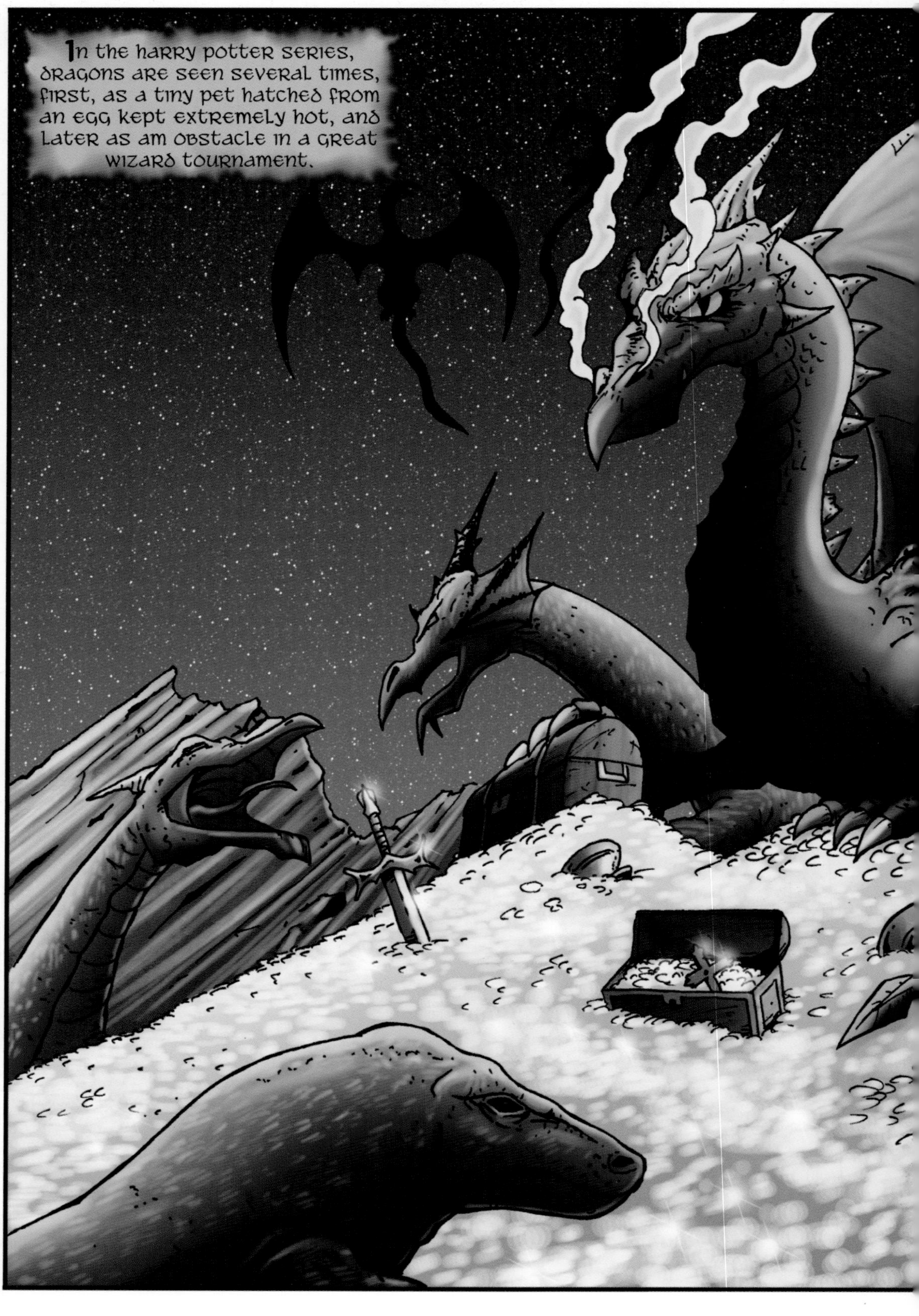
In the harry potter series, dragons are seen several times, first, as a tiny pet hatched from an egg kept extremely hot, and later as am obstacle in a great wizard tournament.

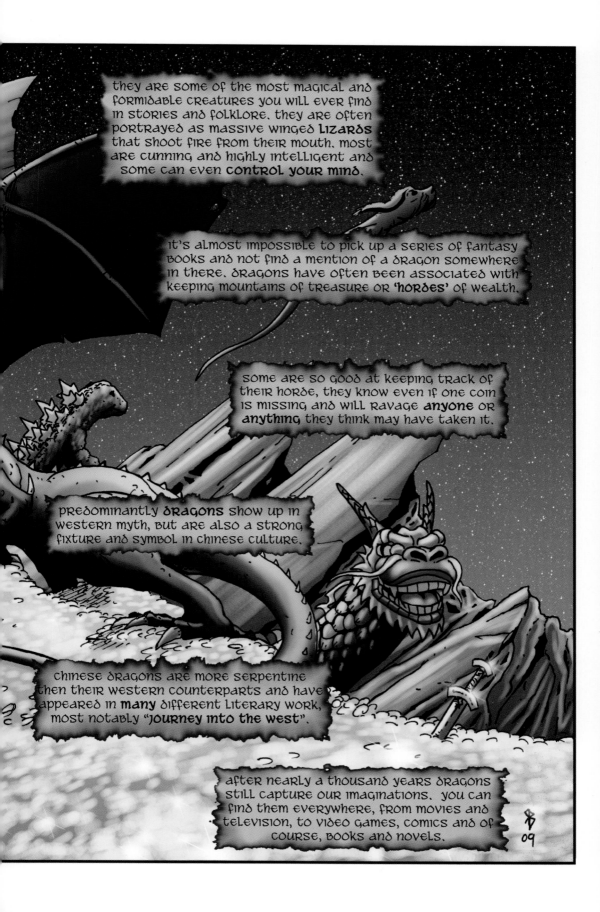

they are some of the most magical and formidable creatures you will ever find in stories and folklore. they are often portrayed as massive winged **lizards** that shoot fire from their mouth. most are cunning and highly intelligent and some can even **control your mind.**

it's almost impossible to pick up a series of fantasy books and not find a mention of a dragon somewhere in there. dragons have often been associated with keeping mountains of treasure or **'hordes'** of wealth.

some are so good at keeping track of their horde, they know even if one coin is missing and will ravage **anyone** or **anything** they think may have taken it.

predominantly **dragons** show up in western myth, but are also a strong fixture and symbol in chinese culture.

chinese dragons are more serpentine then their western counterparts and have appeared in **many** different literary work, most notably "**journey into the west**".

after nearly a thousand years dragons still capture our imaginations. you can find them everywhere, from movies and television, to video games, comics and of course, books and novels.

09

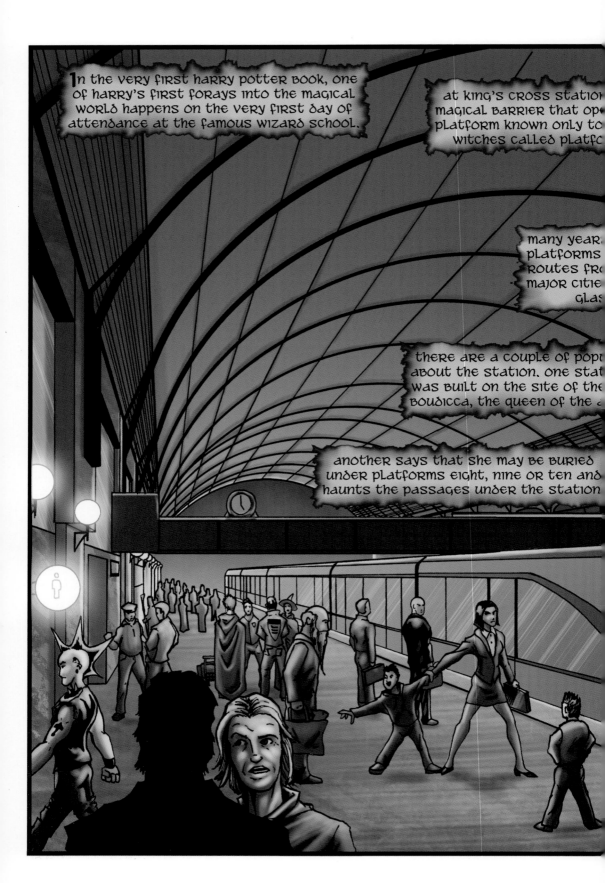

In the very first harry potter book, one of harry's first forays into the magical world happens on the very first day of attendance at the famous wizard school.

at king's cross statio[n] magical barrier that op[en] platform known only to witches called platfo[rm]

many year[s] platforms routes fro[m] major citie[s] glas[gow]

there are a couple of popu[lar] about the station. one stat[ion] was built on the site of the boudicca, the queen of the [...]

another says that she may be buried under platforms eight, nine or ten and haunts the passages under the station

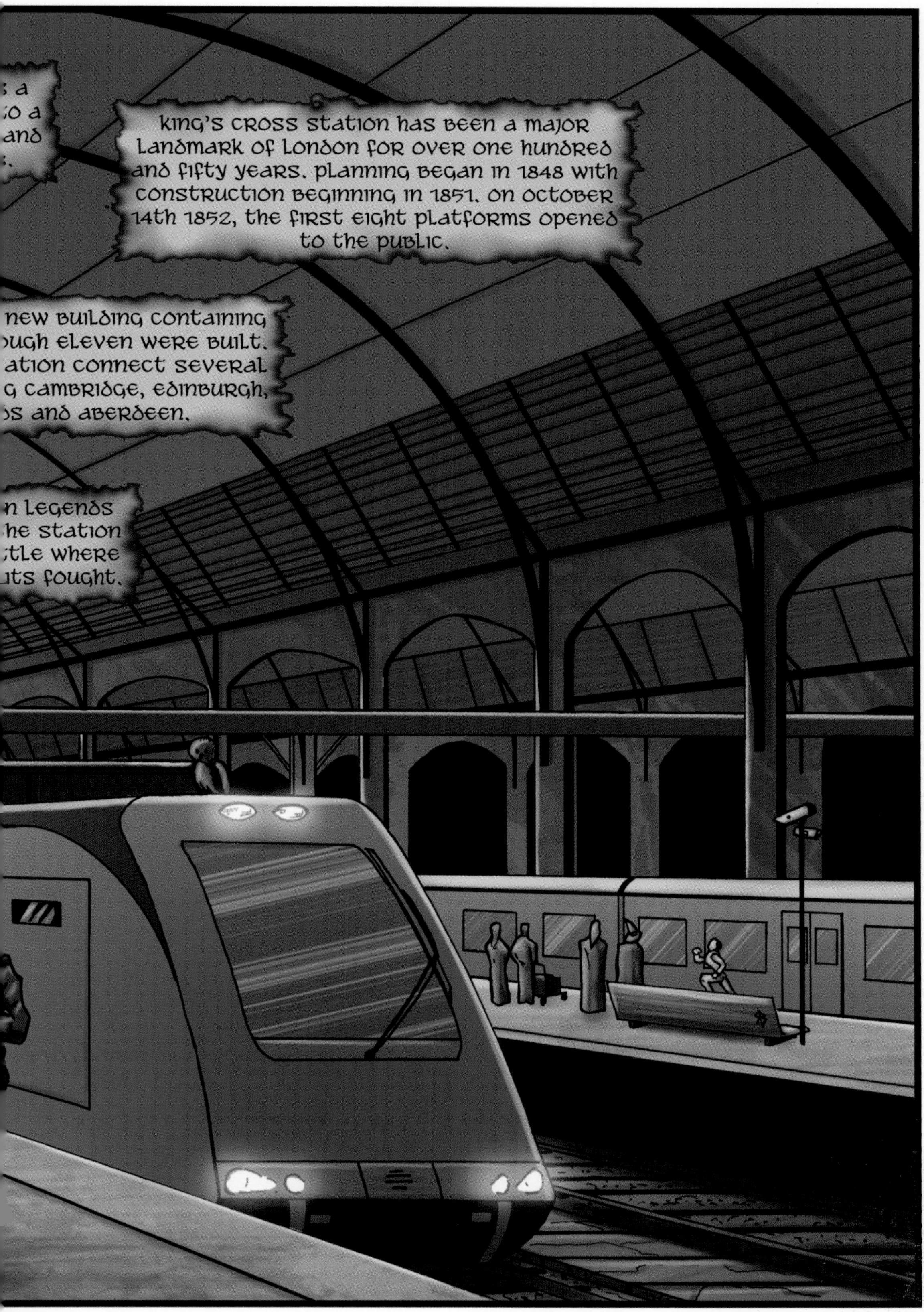
s a
o a
and
King's Cross Station has been a major landmark of London for over one hundred and fifty years. Planning began in 1848 with construction beginning in 1851. On October 14th 1852, the first eight platforms opened to the public.
new building containing
ough eleven were built.
ation connect several
g Cambridge, Edinburgh,
ds and Aberdeen.
n legends
he station
tle where
ts fought.

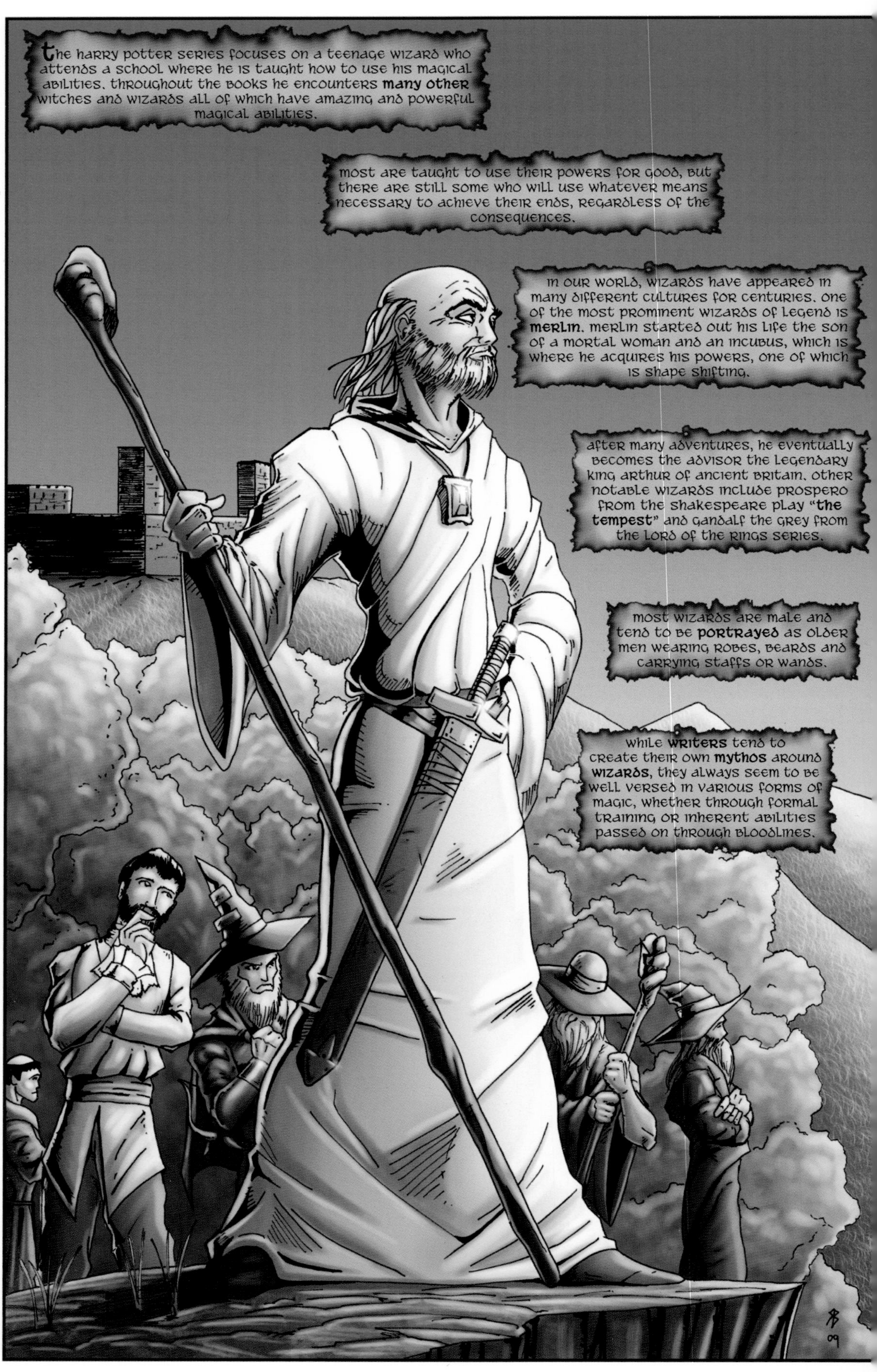
The harry potter series focuses on a teenage wizard who attends a school where he is taught how to use his magical abilities. throughout the books he encounters many other witches and wizards all of which have amazing and powerful magical abilities.
most are taught to use their powers for good, but there are still some who will use whatever means necessary to achieve their ends, regardless of the consequences.
In our world, wizards have appeared in many different cultures for centuries. one of the most prominent wizards of legend is merlin. merlin started out his life the son of a mortal woman and an incubus, which is where he acquires his powers, one of which is shape shifting.
after many adventures, he eventually becomes the advisor the legendary king arthur of ancient britain. other notable wizards include prospero from the shakespeare play "the tempest" and gandalf the grey from the lord of the rings series.
most wizards are male and tend to be portrayed as older men wearing robes, beards and carrying staffs or wands.
while writers tend to create their own mythos around wizards, they always seem to be well versed in various forms of magic, whether through formal training or inherent abilities passed on through bloodlines.
09

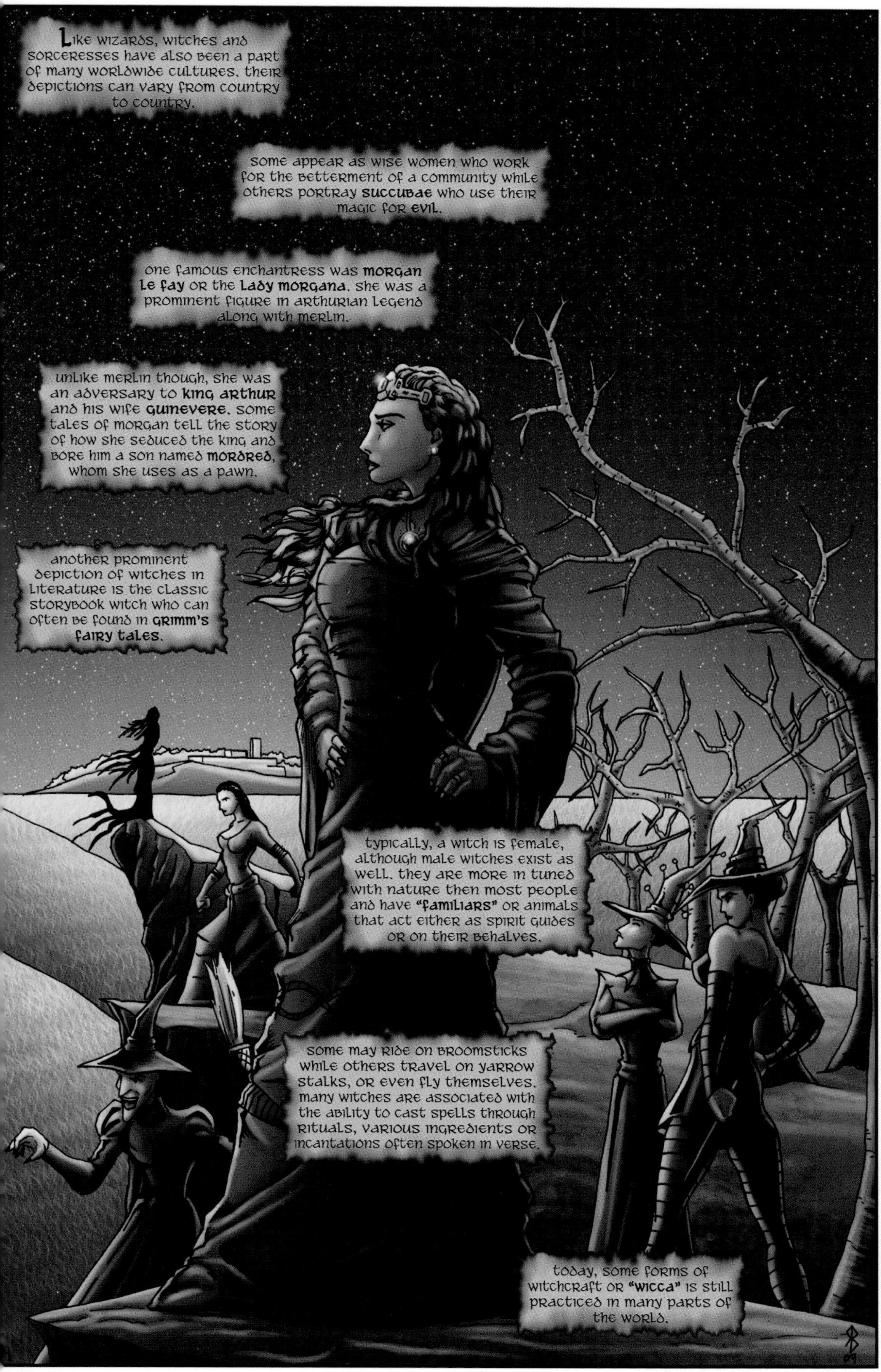
Like wizards, witches and sorceresses have also been a part of many worldwide cultures. their depictions can vary from country to country.
some appear as wise women who work for the betterment of a community while others portray succubae who use their magic for evil.
one famous enchantress was morgan le fay or the lady morgana. she was a prominent figure in arthurian legend along with merlin.
unlike merlin though, she was an adversary to king arthur and his wife guinevere. some tales of morgan tell the story of how she seduced the king and bore him a son named mordred, whom she uses as a pawn.
another prominent depiction of witches in literature is the classic storybook witch who can often be found in grimm's fairy tales.
typically, a witch is female, although male witches exist as well. they are more in tuned with nature then most people and have "familiars" or animals that act either as spirit guides or on their behalves.
some may ride on broomsticks while others travel on yarrow stalks, or even fly themselves. many witches are associated with the ability to cast spells through rituals, various ingredients or incantations often spoken in verse.
today, some forms of witchcraft or "wicca" is still practiced in many parts of the world.

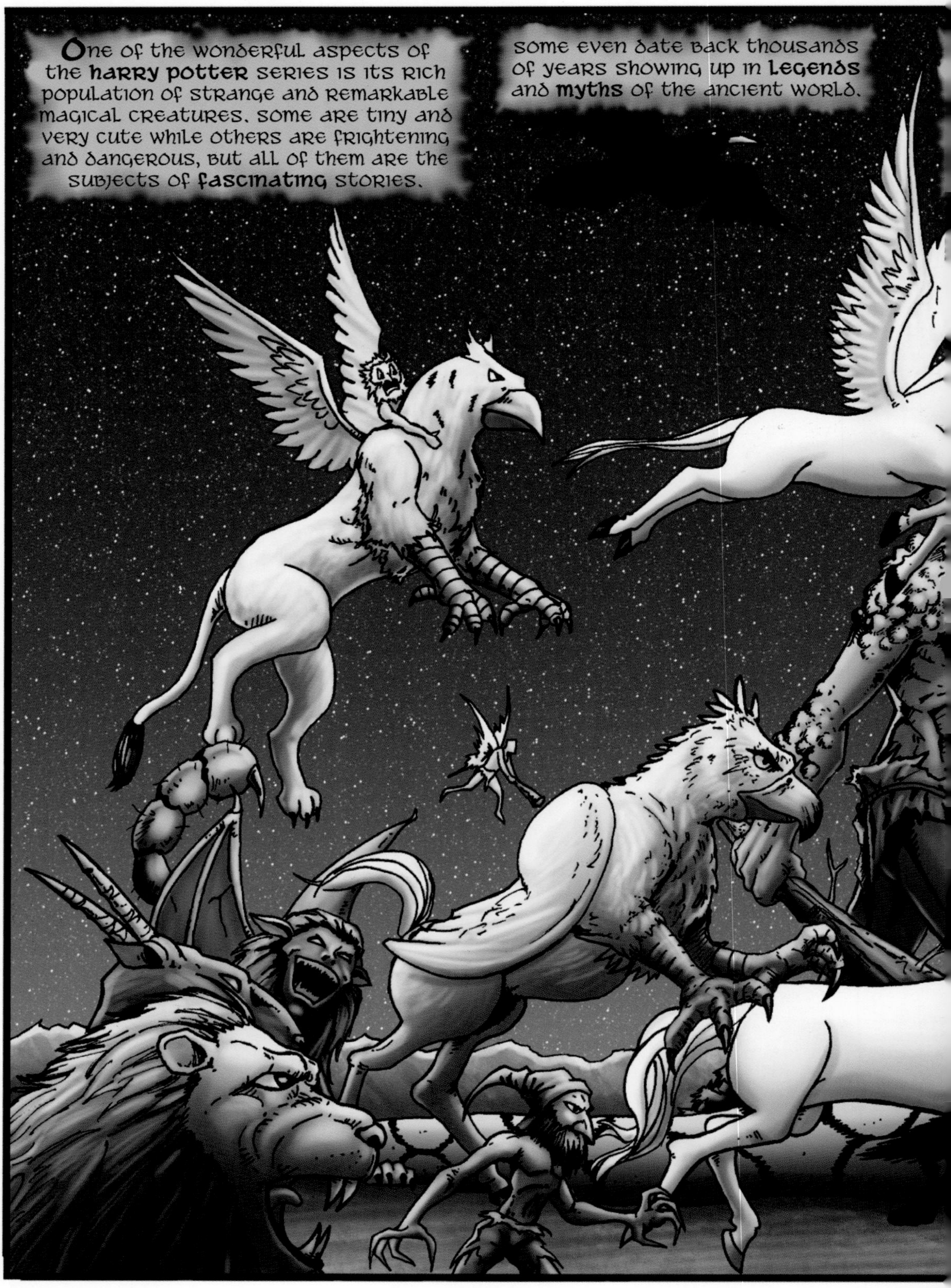
One of the wonderful aspects of the **harry potter** series is its rich population of strange and remarkable magical creatures. some are tiny and very cute while others are frightening and dangerous, but all of them are the subjects of **fascinating** stories.
some even date back thousands of years showing up in **legends** and **myths** of the ancient world.

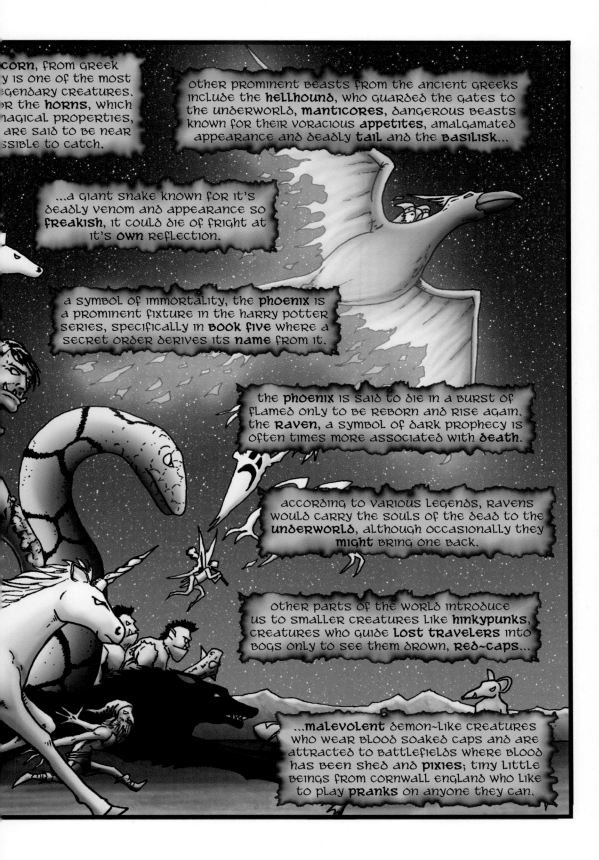

...CORN, FROM GREEK ...Y IS ONE OF THE MOST ...EGENDARY CREATURES, ...R THE **HORNS**, WHICH ...AGICAL PROPERTIES, ...ARE SAID TO BE NEAR ...SSIBLE TO CATCH.

OTHER PROMINENT BEASTS FROM THE ANCIENT GREEKS INCLUDE THE **HELLHOUND**, WHO GUARDED THE GATES TO THE UNDERWORLD, **MANTICORES**, DANGEROUS BEASTS KNOWN FOR THEIR VORACIOUS **APPETITES**, AMALGAMATED APPEARANCE AND DEADLY **TAIL** AND THE **BASILISK**...

...A GIANT SNAKE KNOWN FOR IT'S DEADLY VENOM AND APPEARANCE SO **FREAKISH**, IT COULD DIE OF FRIGHT AT IT'S **OWN** REFLECTION.

A SYMBOL OF IMMORTALITY, THE **PHOENIX** IS A PROMINENT FIXTURE IN THE HARRY POTTER SERIES, SPECIFICALLY IN **BOOK FIVE** WHERE A SECRET ORDER DERIVES ITS **NAME** FROM IT.

THE **PHOENIX** IS SAID TO DIE IN A BURST OF FLAMED ONLY TO BE REBORN AND RISE AGAIN. THE **RAVEN**, A SYMBOL OF DARK PROPHECY IS OFTEN TIMES MORE ASSOCIATED WITH **DEATH**.

ACCORDING TO VARIOUS LEGENDS, RAVENS WOULD CARRY THE SOULS OF THE DEAD TO THE **UNDERWORLD**, ALTHOUGH OCCASIONALLY THEY **MIGHT** BRING ONE BACK.

OTHER PARTS OF THE WORLD INTRODUCE US TO SMALLER CREATURES LIKE **HINKYPUNKS**, CREATURES WHO GUIDE **LOST TRAVELERS** INTO BOGS ONLY TO SEE THEM DROWN, **RED~CAPS**...

...**MALEVOLENT** DEMON-LIKE CREATURES WHO WEAR BLOOD SOAKED CAPS AND ARE ATTRACTED TO BATTLEFIELDS WHERE BLOOD HAS BEEN SHED AND **PIXIES**; TINY LITTLE BEINGS FROM CORNWALL ENGLAND WHO LIKE TO PLAY **PRANKS** ON ANYONE THEY CAN.

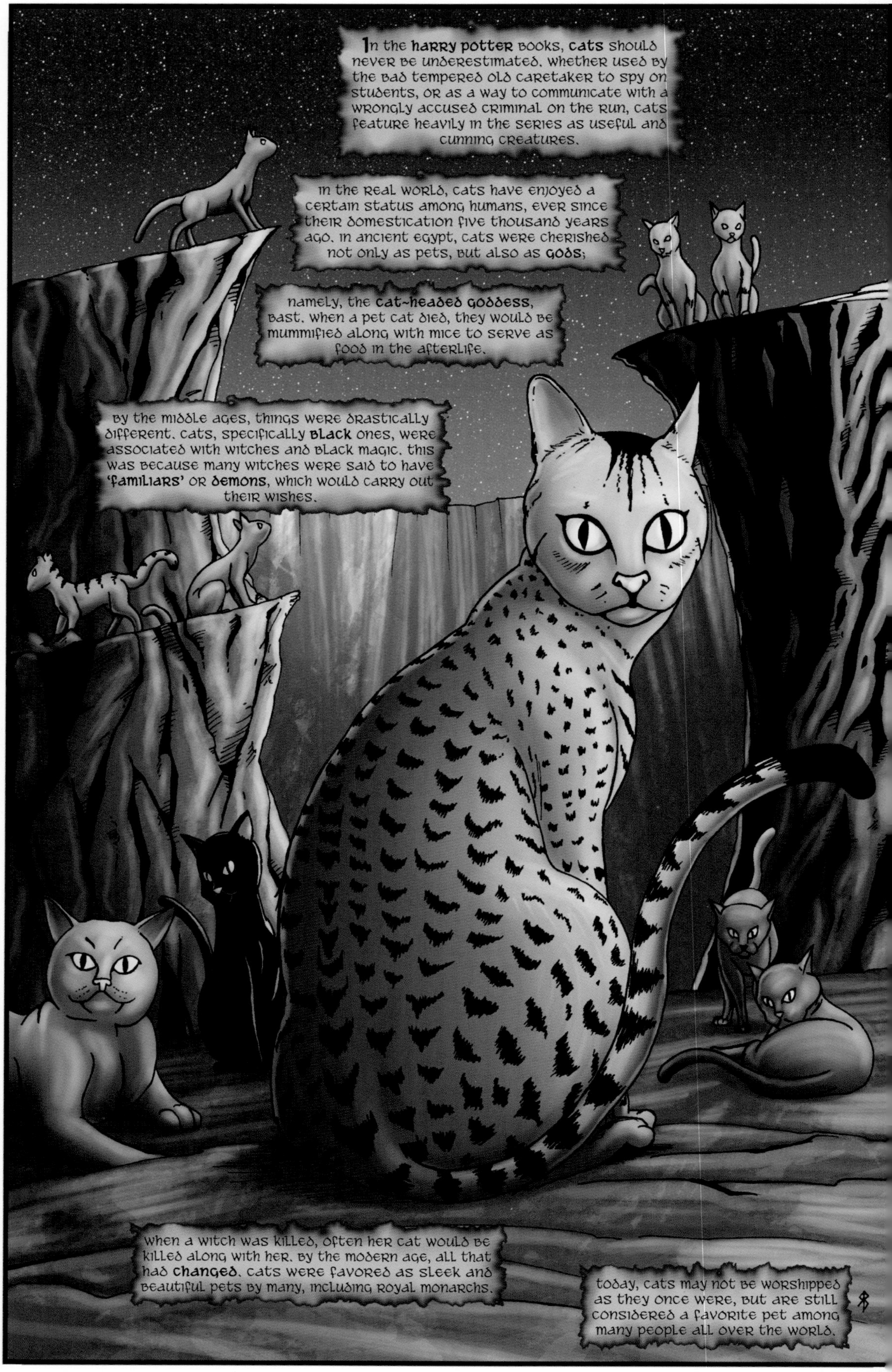
In the harry potter books, cats should never be underestimated. whether used by the bad tempered old caretaker to spy on students, or as a way to communicate with a wrongly accused criminal on the run, cats feature heavily in the series as useful and cunning creatures.
in the real world, cats have enjoyed a certain status among humans, ever since their domestication five thousand years ago. in ancient egypt, cats were cherished not only as pets, but also as gods;
namely, the cat-headed goddess, bast. when a pet cat died, they would be mummified along with mice to serve as food in the afterlife.
by the middle ages, things were drastically different. cats, specifically black ones, were associated with witches and black magic. this was because many witches were said to have 'familiars' or demons, which would carry out their wishes.
when a witch was killed, often her cat would be killed along with her. by the modern age, all that had changed. cats were favored as sleek and beautiful pets by many, including royal monarchs.
today, cats may not be worshipped as they once were, but are still considered a favorite pet among many people all over the world.

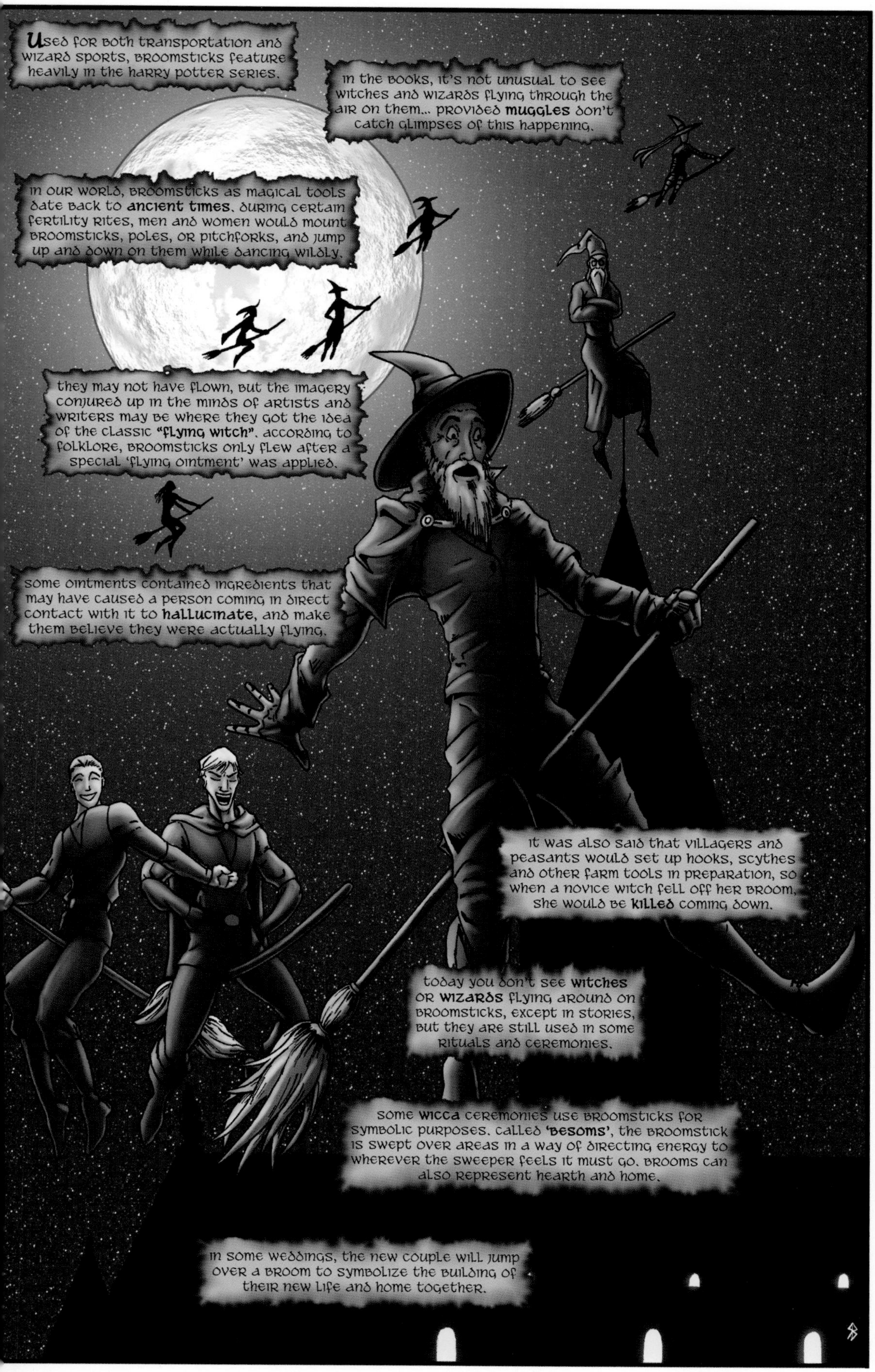
Used for both transportation and wizard sports, broomsticks feature heavily in the harry potter series.
in the books, it's not unusual to see witches and wizards flying through the air on them... provided muggles don't catch glimpses of this happening.
in our world, broomsticks as magical tools date back to ancient times. during certain fertility rites, men and women would mount broomsticks, poles, or pitchforks, and jump up and down on them while dancing wildly.
they may not have flown, but the imagery conjured up in the minds of artists and writers may be where they got the idea of the classic "flying witch". according to folklore, broomsticks only flew after a special 'flying ointment' was applied.
some ointments contained ingredients that may have caused a person coming in direct contact with it to hallucinate, and make them believe they were actually flying.
it was also said that villagers and peasants would set up hooks, scythes and other farm tools in preparation, so when a novice witch fell off her broom, she would be killed coming down.
today you don't see witches or wizards flying around on broomsticks, except in stories, but they are still used in some rituals and ceremonies.
some wicca ceremonies use broomsticks for symbolic purposes. called 'besoms', the broomstick is swept over areas in a way of directing energy to wherever the sweeper feels it must go. brooms can also represent hearth and home.
in some weddings, the new couple will jump over a broom to symbolize the building of their new life and home together.

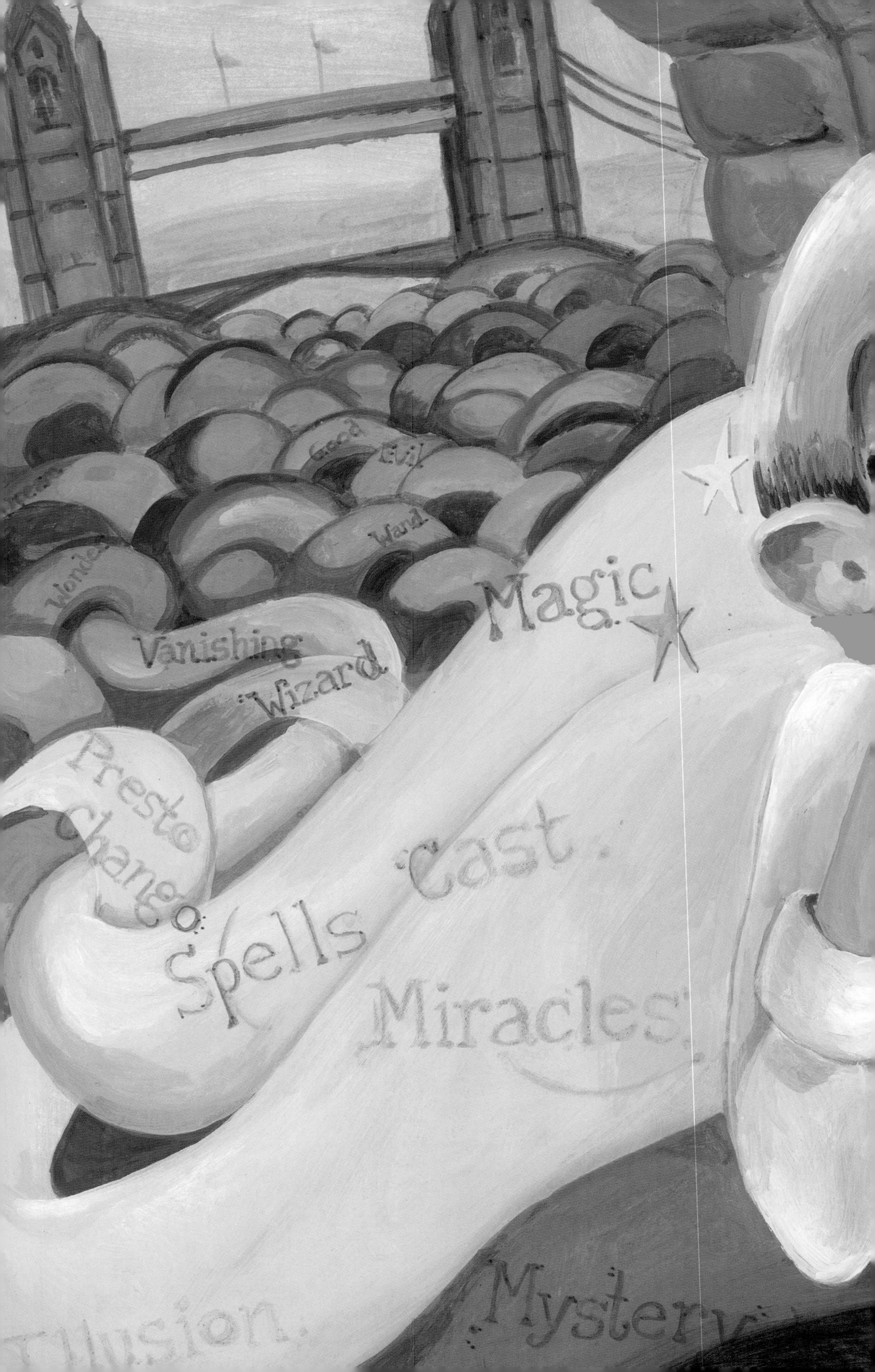
Good
Evil
Wand
Vanishing
Wizard
Magic
Presto
chango
Spells
Cast
Miracles
Illusion

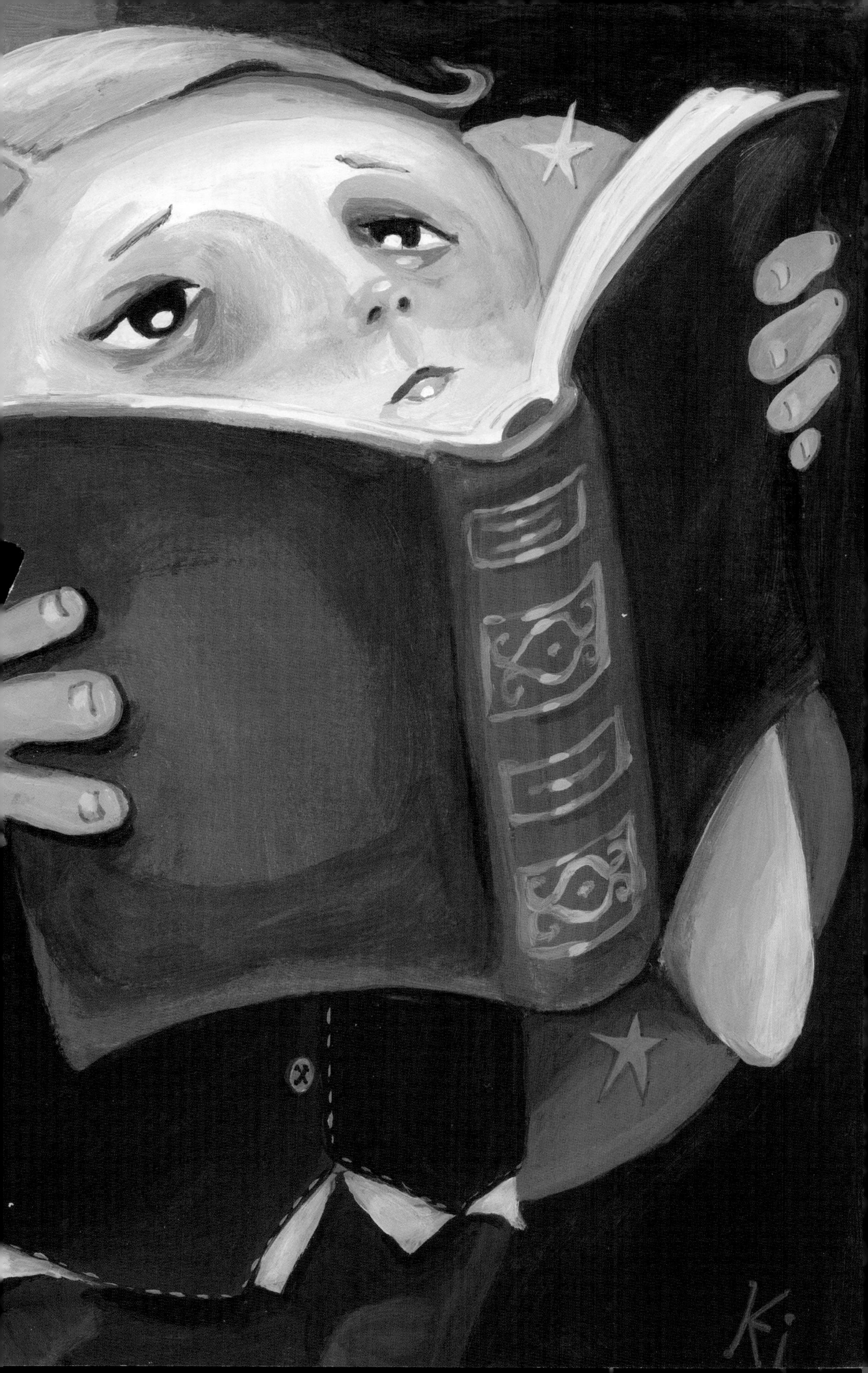

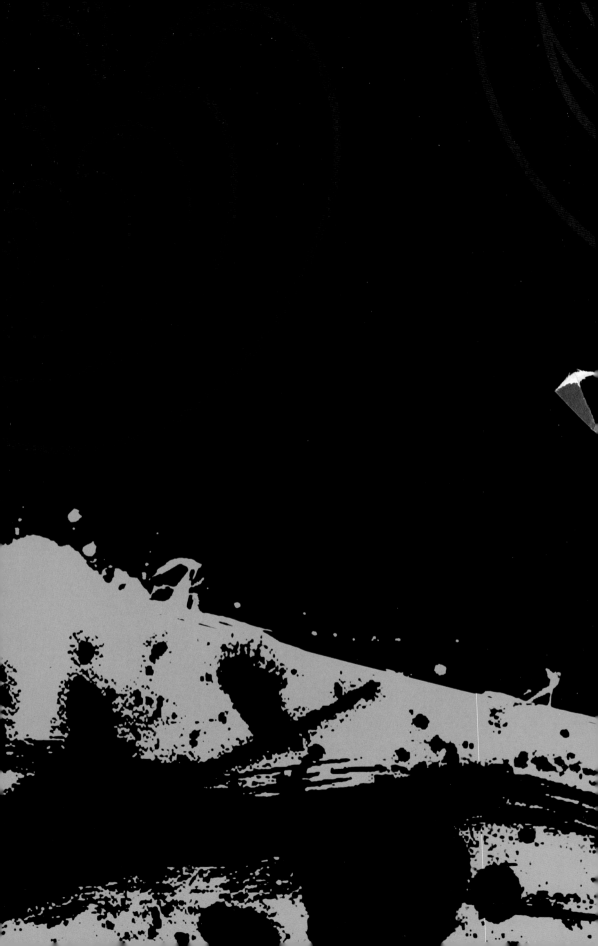